ZACHARIAH'S STORY

LOVE WINS

FRED HAMPTON

WESTBOW
PRESS®
A DIVISION OF THOMAS NELSON
& ZONDERVAN

Copyright © 2020 Fred Hampton.

All rights reserved. No part of this book may be used or reproduced by any means, graphic, electronic, or mechanical, including photocopying, recording, taping or by any information storage retrieval system without the written permission of the author except in the case of brief quotations embodied in critical articles and reviews.

This book is a work of non-fiction. Unless otherwise noted, the author and the publisher make no explicit guarantees as to the accuracy of the information contained in this book and in some cases, names of people and places have been altered to protect their privacy.

WestBow Press books may be ordered through booksellers or by contacting:

WestBow Press
A Division of Thomas Nelson & Zondervan
1663 Liberty Drive
Bloomington, IN 47403
www.westbowpress.com
1 (866) 928-1240

Because of the dynamic nature of the Internet, any web addresses or links contained in this book may have changed since publication and may no longer be valid. The views expressed in this work are solely those of the author and do not necessarily reflect the views of the publisher, and the publisher hereby disclaims any responsibility for them.

Any people depicted in stock imagery provided by Getty Images are models, and such images are being used for illustrative purposes only. Certain stock imagery © Getty Images.

Scripture quotations are from the ESV® Bible (The Holy Bible, English Standard Version®), copyright © 2001 by Crossway, a publishing ministry of Good News Publishers. Used by permission. All rights reserved.

ISBN: 978-1-9736-8382-7 (sc)
ISBN: 978-1-9736-8383-4 (hc)
ISBN: 978-1-9736-8381-0 (e)

Library of Congress Control Number: 2020900630

Print information available on the last page.

WestBow Press rev. date: 01/13/2020

CONTENTS

Foreword...vii

Preface... xiii

Chapter 1 Twenty-Seven Children in Ten Years............. 1

Chapter 2 He Almost Didn't Stay.......................... 9

Chapter 3 Choosing to Live 15

Chapter 4 Is This for Real, or Is It a Dream? 21

Chapter 5 Community, We Are Not Alone 35

Chapter 6 The Courage to Suffer Well 51

Chapter 7 A Smooth Rock................................69

Chapter 8 Babies and Cheese Fries.......................81

Chapter 9 Just a Guy 91

Chapter 10 Girlfriends 105

Chapter 11 Play Ball 113

Chapter 12 Killing Zombies 119

Chapter 13 Walk and Talk................................127

Chapter 14 Maybe the Ending Is the Beginning............139

Chapter 15 Last Things...................................147

Epilogue..159

About the Author...165

FOREWORD

I've gotten to know Fred Hampton well over the past few years. I met him about four years ago, we go to the same church, and we have worked together on the training of lay counselors at our church. Even better, we have become friends, sharing meals and fellowship together.

We met a few years after the death of the son, whom this book is about. As a result, I never got to meet Zachariah in person. But after reading the book, I wish I had. I'm so thankful that Fred made the decision to write up some stories about him and many of his experiences with him. Zach had some significant disabilities, including some intellectual limitations, but he was often a joyful soul, and Fred allowed himself to enter into his son's world and play with him there. As a result, I found that there is something mysteriously profound in these pages, made so by the strange beauty of Zachariah's disabilities combined with Fred's humility.

Also, what makes this book such a treasure is the fact that Fred is a therapist. Consequently, he walks us through these stories with the wisdom of one who knows a lot about the healing journey, what to look for along the way, and how to facilitate it. To serve the reader in this way, Fred had to open up and share some of his journey with us, including a fair amount of pain. That's never easy. I read this with my wife. Thanks, my friend, for letting us both get to know you better and for role-modeling for us what the journey looks like! May this book bring other readers a little further down the road of their own healing journey, as it did us.

Eric L. Johnson, PhD,
Professor of Christian Psychology, Houston Baptist University,
Director, Gideon Institute for Christian
Psychology and Counseling

***

In spite of the fact that Fred Hampton and I have both had long careers in the same city treating many (and sometimes the same) people for emotional, spiritual, and interpersonal suffering, I met him only four years ago when grace connected us through the sharing of the same office building. For decades we'd shared some of the same friends and colleagues; amazingly we'd even attended the same church. But we didn't have any idea that we were all along perfectly suited to become close friends until we began to work out of the same address.

Maybe it was when he invited me to ride with him to Lexington for a football game. Possibly it was before. But somewhere early in our budding brotherhood, Fred shared with me a few details about the remarkable gift and the crushing loss of his adoptive son, Zachariah. In that first year I knew him, Fred couldn't speak or hear Zachariah's name without tearing up. With time and through a number of recounting, both with Fred and with his dear wife, Marchelle, I began to grasp more and more how Zachariah had become a full-fledged member of the Hampton family. Even so, it wasn't until I read a draft of this moving book that I could begin to understand who Zachariah was, how he had transformed the family that had rescued him and enlivened the many lives with whom he came in contact, and why his sudden, premature departure had so completely leveled and overwhelmed his parents.

Zachariah was a long-odds infant when he came to be fostered by the Hamptons. Injured and neglected both pre- and postnatally, it seemed everything had gone against him and his chances for survival. That is, until he was placed with a Hampton family which, along with the two parents, included

Kristie and her younger brother, Josh (Bailey). In this nurturing environment, Zachariah would go from balancing precariously on the edge of survival to a robust thriving. And although he had several physical and neurological deficits with which he and his family would contend, these challenges could in no way mask a huge and enlivening spirit that grew to envelop not just those at the Hampton home base but also a forever growing circle of fortunate people whose lives came into lucky contact with his.

Like some rare celestial happening, Zachariah was a once-in-a-lifetime phenomenon. I, and most of you reading this, were sadly enough at the wrong place to witness this comet of a spirit who was blazingly here and then too suddenly gone. But, oh, what an impact his presence has had on the lives and spirits of his adoptive family, his church, his school, and countless strangers who chanced to meet him during his cowboy travels out West in the family's trusty RV. What the world calls disabilities, Zachariah turned into enabling, allowing him to never lose childhood's wonderful capacity for fantasy. Whether he was playing a policeman, cowboy, or rock 'n' roll drummer, he was always decked out in the full regalia, fitting the role he was inhabiting.

I've come to understand that what made Zachariah most special (as in special *deeds*, not special needs) was his boundless capacity for engaging in relationship. Over the past several decades, my profession has come to understand that all adoptive children and their adoptive parents will confront and often struggle mightily through painful issues of attachment, the capacity to engage with others in mutually beneficial, nondestructive relationship. However we try to explain it, Zachariah seems to have arrived here with a rare and beautiful gift for attachment that raised the lumens and brightened colors for all those who came to know him.

I invite you to read on in order that Fred's easy style and emotional honesty can give you a sense of what you missed if you didn't know Zachariah. It's the story of a boy ever so fortunate to have been enveloped by a Hampton family eager to follow his lead into a new, larger way of living. It's the tale of a magical synergism that evolved between the adoptee and his adopters such that all parties were empowered to utterly flourish as never before. It's the stuff of fairy tales, and it's a wake-up call for a broken, polarized world, showing us that this is who and what we all were born to be to one another.

Robert H. Stewart, MD
October 1, 2019

PREFACE

Written sometime in the late '80s

Last night, when I looked at the potential of death and this unthinkable loss, a burning question haunted me. What if one of my children died? Would I continue to believe and trust my relationship with God? I decided I would no longer believe.

This morning, as I consider my decision, I realize the conditional nature of my faith. What does it say about the strength and security of my faith? Should my belief and love of God be dependent on my external circumstances? The quick and easy answer is no, but the more honest answer reveals my human condition. I have never really resolved this question.

Do other people struggle like I do, or are they able to live with more clarity and absolute belief? It often appears that these answers are so much easier to resolve for others. Perhaps this is true, or maybe I simply keep pushing these questions when others find them unnecessary. At any rate, my questions still linger and influence my spiritual pilgrimage. Perhaps some of the answers will not be found in the places I've looked. I want certainty about these questions to calm my fear and doubt.

This journey of what is so difficult to ask and even more difficult to answer can exist only within the context of faith. Faith holds the space where the answers are provided or where I become comfortable with the unanswered. I suppose faith is the acceptance of things we cannot always understand or change, and the willingness in spite of this to remain steadfast, trust our journey, and accept the obstacles that living presents. If the kind of tragedy I gave thought to would occur, I may stop believing, and with the lack of belief, I know I will slowly stop breathing. It is at this place that God will reappear.

Thirty Years Later ...

This journal entry lay in a folder, collecting dust among some other writings I had long forgotten about. It reveals my struggle as a young man with the questions of life and death. Where and how do we hold onto faith in the midst of devastating loss? Those words were written long before a malnourished little boy showed up and changed all of us who knew and loved him. The unimaginable has happened, and I am exposed. What I believe and where I will put my trust will determine whether I will move forward and how.

I want to tell his story because his is such a remarkable story to tell. I want to tell you some of my story not because it is so remarkable, but because it would be hard to tell you his story without telling you some of mine.

Zachariah Nathaniel Hampton passed away on August 29, 2014.

Many people with good intentions approached me, saying, "Life will never be the same," or, "You will never get over this." Yes, I will never be the same—and the truth is, I never want to be the same. To be the same would not honor Zachariah's life. It is important that some good things come out of what has been so tragic. I don't want to be a casualty. I want to be a man who courageously faces his loss and who doesn't lose faith. Zachariah lived in the moment, and his passing has brought me to this moment. I am much less afraid, and I have gratitude amid this incredible heartache. I am writing because it is part of my healing, and I am writing because I want you to know about this amazing young man.

Twenty-Seven Children in Ten Years

WE HAD CONSIDERED BECOMING FOSTER PARENTS FOR several years. Marchelle and I had been married for thirteen years when we made the decision. Our twelve-year-old daughter, Kristie, and our ten-year-old son, Josh, were equally excited about this new adventure. We were all excited and naive. We had no idea the heartache and suffering that would follow.

Twenty-seven children in ten years. Some came for a few days, and some stayed for a few years. These broken children mirrored some of our brokenness. Marchelle and I both came from difficult childhoods. Marchelle suffered abuse as a child. Not unlike these children in our care, she came into a world that neglected and abused her. Hers is a story of amazing courage and faith, running away from home at an early age to escape the abuse. By holding onto hope when hope was not in sight, she found her way through suffering. It was not in a context of hopelessness but one where hope and faith existed. Within this space, she was able to grieve the abuse she had suffered. Grief was no longer something to fear because of the grace she had found. She did not waste her pain but asked God to speak into it and heal what was broken in her life. The open wound has been replaced by scars—evidence of the healing and transforming power of God's love. She has taught and continues to teach me so much about what it means to love and forgive. She loves others with such courage and sacrifice. God brought these children to us knowing Marchelle would love them back to life.

My story was different yet similar. I too came from a dysfunctional family. Both my parents were alcoholics. My father was a very kind and compassionate man. He had a wonderful sense of humor, and laughter infused our home. My father loved animals and passed on this love to me. We had dogs, chickens, ducks, horses, and a cow named Daisy. When I was young, I remember staying up all night with my dad tending to a group of sick baby chicks. The rooster and my father had a real power struggle. I recall seeing my father being chased by the rooster, only to be saved by jumping on the hood of his car.

As kind as he was, there was also a great deal of passivity and avoidance. I never saw him angry, and he avoided conflict with my mother. His father had been an alcoholic who had gone on drinking binges for days and spent what little money the family had. Toward the end of my father's life, he shared more stories—many I had not heard before. He shared that on several occasions as a young boy, he'd found his father passed out in the field, unable to make it to the house after drinking all night. My father was a survivor; he never unpacked his emotional baggage. Few did from that generation. He was a good man with a gentle and compassionate spirit. He loved me unconditionally, and I am grateful.

What he failed to do was protect me from my mother. She was a fearful and jealous woman. I know she loved me, but I am not convinced she liked me. When she was angry, she withheld approval. When intoxicated, she was verbally abusive. I recall lying in bed and praying I would go to sleep before they had too much to drink. I would often pray they both would give up alcohol.

Like most, Marchelle and I were wounded people attempting to find our way. We met at Campbellsville University. She was an incoming freshman, and I was starting my senior year. We met at the yearly picnic intended to welcome new and returning students. We quickly became friends. We both were looking for some sense of belonging, and we found it in each other and in the small Christian school we were attending. I believe God brought us together.

We started hanging out at a married couple's house off campus. The couple was caring for a small farm in exchange for being allowed to live in an old farmhouse, which had little insulation and was heated by a wood stove. It was a special time in our lives; we had good friends and a supportive Christian community, and we grew increasingly fond of each other. My roommate, believing that Marchelle and I were just good friends, decided he would pursue a romantic relationship with her. This resulted in an honest conversation with my roommate and a late-night walk around campus with Marchelle. We both confessed our feelings for the other and began dating. We had a very short courtship and were married outside a small country church.

For a while, our love steamed ahead, full of passion and adventure. Children came quickly. Kristie was born ten months after we were married, and Josh followed three years later. Eventually, we discovered that in our bliss, there was also some fear and uncertainty. Marriage requires a great deal of emotional unpacking. It does not take long in marriage for one's woundedness to be revealed. Marriage, for those who recognize it, is a people-growing machine. It requires us to find the courage to look into our own lives.

We committed to each other and began the journey. We were determined to do things differently. We had grown up in a generation that was beginning to encourage the unpacking of emotional baggage. After some time as a social worker, I completed a graduate degree and began a career as a therapist. I recognized that the effectiveness of my work partly depended on my own healing. Early on, both Marchelle and I worked hard to heal our wounds from childhood. We battled the lies that were birthed in the abuse and driven by the shame we had suffered in our childhoods.

None of us get cured, but we do get better if we walk in the right direction. We all carry some emotional and spiritual wounds into our adult lives. We needed to attend to our woundedness. To not do this would leave us vulnerable to living with maladaptive coping mechanisms, which provide no more than survival. The truth is we all carry forward the stories of our lives. No matter how much denial, avoidance, and self-medicating we employ, we cannot escape our stories. Our righteous work is to give voice to our wounds, remove the shame, and confront the lies. God invites us into truth and transforming grace. This grace becomes a crucible where mercy abounds.

I had spent some time earlier as a child protective services worker, so I had some understanding of the challenges that would come with fostering abused and neglected children. There was obvious concern about how becoming a foster family might negatively impact Kristie and Josh. Love, affection, and protection would need to be spread out a little wider. All four of us got on board and were equally excited. All of us would take part, watching life being breathed into what was once abused and abandoned. We made the decision to take only younger children, in hopes that Kristie and Josh would be influential in their lives.

Our first foster child was a newborn baby girl whose mother had abused several of her other children. It was decided she was unfit to care for this child. We cared for her during the first four months of her life. We witnessed her new adoptive mom seeing her for the first time and beginning the journey of being her mom. This was followed by two siblings, two and four years old, who came and stayed for two years. The day they left, we were heartbroken. I stayed home from work; Kristie and Josh stayed home from school. We grieved and had done our best to protect our hearts. This protection proved to be impossible because if you were really going to show up, your heart would be exposed.

Our hearts continued to be broken as children came and left. But there were also many funny moments caring for these precious children. There were three little boys who arrived with these angelic-looking faces. Two of them, one age four and one age five, had already spent much of their lives in foster care. We tucked them in the first night only to find our home trashed the next morning. The pantry and refrigerator had been emptied and deposited throughout our home.

It was not unusual for many of the children who came our way to immediately begin referring to Marchelle and me as Mommy and Daddy. They seemed to be comforted by this. Perhaps the fantasy allowed for the denial of all the heartache and uncertainty in their lives. There were two sisters, aged four and five, who had never been to church. We told them they would learn about God and Jesus and meet a lot of kind people. When an elderly gentleman greeted them at the door on their first day at church, the five-year-old excitedly asked if that man was Jesus.

All of the children who came our way had suffered some sort of abuse and neglect. Some were returned to unstable environments. Most had suffered to the extent that they had given up on trusting and believing they could be loved. Their emotional walls were up, and survival was their primary means of coping. We witnessed toddlers who, when they suffered a scraped knee or bruised elbow, would become angry rather than risk the exposure of being hurt. Vulnerability was already viewed as a direct path to further hurt. So much of the abuse they had suffered was experienced in isolation.

These children were wounded physically, emotionally, and spiritually. Their pain had not been validated, and when hurt is experienced in isolation, it impacts a child's ability to believe. "It has not been okay, and therefore it will never be okay" becomes the armor surrounding the heart. The ability to trust and receive comfort is severely damaged. We did our best to love them back to being able to trust and to a willingness to be loved.

I have been a therapist for more than thirty years, and I have come to believe that the deepest wound in our lives is spiritual. When pain is not validated and comfort is not received, there is a deep spiritual wound. It affects our ability to believe, trust, and seek comfort. Security becomes about control, and our willingness to love is damaged. Whether conscious or not, exposure of feelings or needs is seen as another hurt. Most of the children who came to us had already given up on being loved. Their walls were up, and survival meant the protection of the heart. Their little spirits had been damaged, but they were surviving. They came and they left, twenty-six in all. Then a little boy showed up whose life changed us forever.

He Almost Didn't Stay

THE FIRST TIME I LAID EYES ON HIM, HE WAS NINE MONTHS old. I had come in from a long day at work knowing I would meet our new foster child. I was shocked at what I saw—he looked like a malnourished little bird. He made no sounds and looked like living or dying was yet to be decided. Technically, he was considered a "failure to thrive" baby. When he was first discovered by Child Protective Services, he had already begun to give up on living. He had suffered significant emotional and physical trauma—head trauma due to being kicked by one of his mother's boyfriends, and traumatic neglect as a result of being left unattended. When the authorities found him, he was dirty, suffering from a fever, and living in filthy conditions. He was dying in a playpen. Somewhere along the way, he had suffered a stroke and had some paralysis. By the time he arrived in our care, there were multiple diagnoses, only to be followed by more diagnoses and a bleak prognosis.

We were told he would probably never walk or develop the ability to speak. The kind of trauma he had suffered had impacted him physically, emotionally, and spiritually. His entrance into the world was unwelcome; his body was damaged and his faith was crushed. He had lost the will to live. When I looked into his eyes that first night, there was no response. I wondered what he thought and what he believed.

He was different than all the other children who had come into our home. He had no one. He was never going to be returned to his mother, and there was uncertainty about who his father was. He was alone. Given his prognosis, there was concern about finding him an adoptive home. Like all the other times, we set our sights on loving him, caring for him, and preparing him for a permanent home.

His name then was Christopher. We later changed his name to Zachariah, which I will explain later. I have no idea how he got his first name. I never met his mother or father, so I have no idea whether that name was given much thought or love. What I do know is that Christopher came into a world that was unprepared for him. The story we were told was that his mother was a chronic alcohol and drug abuser. She also had a long history of choosing violent men and having multiple children removed from her home after their exposure to domestic violence.

Several years after Christopher came into our home, we were informed that she had been killed by one of her boyfriends. She was broken and wounded and certainly not prepared or capable of being a mother. Something must have happened when she was young. At some point early on, she must have suffered a betrayal similar to the one to which she exposed her children. What sort of abuse, neglect, and abandonment had she experienced? How much love, if any, had she ever received? We are all wounded in some way; it is our human condition. I wonder whether she could express her suffering. How did she carry her loss? Given how she lived and how she died, I believe she denied, avoided, and medicated her pain with a multitude of compulsive behaviors. She probably ran out of hope at an early age; her faith crumbled, and she gave up on God or anyone else saving her.

I thought about her in the early days after my son passed away. I wondered whether she ever lay awake at night and cried about her losses, and whether she felt anything close to the pain I was feeling. It seems she could not hold a space for the losses she had suffered. I questioned and had fears that I could not hold a space for it either. The suffering was too great.

In a way I don't quite understand, I experienced more sympathy for this woman than I'd ever had before. We both had suffered devastating losses. We were different, but we were the same. She had allowed her son, my son, to be abused, abandoned, and left for dead. It was strange to me at the time that I felt very little judgment toward her. My grief had brought me to a new place. In the midst of devastating grief, God had provided me with compassion that was both confusing and liberating. I recognized then, and I believe now, that it was grace.

I was beginning to understand and experience grace in a new way. I used to love throwing the word around; it felt good and sounded good. I was broken, and surrendering was the only real option if I was to live this life. "I can't, but God can" is that precious spot where much is revealed and life is liberated. Although grace is a gift, it is not without requirement. It demands, in the words of twelve-step recovery, to finally live life on life's terms. We don't get only what feels good—we also get the hard stuff. Grace exists in a context where acceptance and surrender abound. This newfound experience of grace must involve the integration of my suffering. Because suffering is inevitable, grace becomes the container that holds my suffering. Suffering becomes that place where God does some of his best work. Grief requires suffering, and suffering requires surrender for grace to show up in a transformative way.

I desperately wanted my old life back, the life when Zachariah was still with us. I also wanted to hold on to what grace was providing. I tried, and am still trying, to live with my loss and invite grace to transform me in the midst of my suffering. Transforming grace is not dependent on a feeling or an experience; it is anchored and secure in a context of faith.

Choosing to Live

THE EARLY MONTHS WITH CHRISTOPHER WERE BUSY WITH various doctor appointments and visits from physical, occupational, and speech therapists. For the most part, he was nonresponsive to physical touch or human interaction. It was often painful to watch as he withdrew into himself and self-soothed. He would often rock as a way of comforting himself. When he was frightened or confused, he would fall to the ground and curl up in a fetal position. Clearly the world, his world, had not been safe. He was a trauma survivor and was doing no more than surviving.

Ever so slowly, he began to show signs of connecting with his world. Early on, when placed in a high chair, he would be almost catatonic as someone fed him. Josh and I would often dance around him, singing and making noise in an effort to reach him. He began to utter sounds, and I will never forget this one moment. Josh and I were play wrestling in the kitchen next to him. He was in his high chair, and we heard, "Ga." We froze, called Marchelle and Kristie into the room, and waited for the next "ga." It happened again, and we all danced around the high chair. He looked shocked by the fact that he had made a sound and all these people were dancing around him.

Christopher's first word carried a lot of meaning and was the first tangible evidence of the externalization of need. He was beginning to trust that if he put his needs out there, his world would not reject or hurt him. Such a simple act, yet it held tremendous significance. He was beginning to breathe in the sustenance of life. He was becoming open to the possibility that he was loved and he was lovable. He started sitting in front of the refrigerator when he was thirsty or hungry.

He also began to respond to touch. In the very early days and months of his life, touch often meant physical pain. Christopher was now experiencing the comfort and assurance loving touch provides. Where once he would resist and become agitated, he began to let go and take the love we offered. As he began to believe, we saw more and more physical and emotional change. He had suffered a stroke prior to living with us, and there was paralysis on one side of his face. We began to notice that his body was more relaxed, his eyes would look at us rather than look away, and he began to smile.

I remember the first time he laughed; his face was all distorted, and a strange sound came out of his mouth. Once again we all celebrated, and once again he looked shocked and confused. He was smiling; it was the weirdest and most beautiful smile I have ever seen. This beautiful smile would eventually turn into laughter and a precious sense of humor. Those were good days; he was actively joining his foster family.

Kristie and Josh were such a vital part of his development. Their energy and involvement breathed new life into his broken spirit. Not unlike most families, there were nicknames; he was "boo" and "critter." Slowly, his spirit began to show up; early on, his defense against unwanted attention was to spit. He would take in a mouthful of water and hurl it toward his victim. His accuracy was amazing. Josh would compare him to a camel, which employs the same weaponry.

His tears were further evidence of his recovery. In the early days, he would moan, and there would be no visible tears. But then tears began to show up. His tears were evidence that his spirit was awakening, and he was having some sense of mattering. I think about my grandchildren and how, from the very beginning, they knew they mattered. Their arrival into this world was met with celebration, love, and protection. What a tremendous gift to know, perhaps even in the womb, one is loved. How terrifying it must have been to come into a world that immediately rejected and hurt him. How alone he was, and how terrified he must have felt. No wonder his spiritual, emotional, and physical self began to die.

The power of "I am glad you are here" and "I will protect you" is the foundation of faith. Something so simple and so natural for most of us has such a profound impact on the birthing of faith. There was a deep spiritual injury in his life that had profoundly affected his willingness to believe. Hope and faith are born out of unconditional love and acceptance. When our sadness, fear, and even anger are met with understanding, protection, and love, then hope is born. A life without hope is a dark and marginal existence.

There were many physical challenges. Christopher was legally blind; he had no vision in one of his eyes and the other was significantly compromised. He had very poor circulation, and in the winter season we would have to be careful when exposing him to cold temperatures. He had mild cerebral palsy, which affected his mobility. He got around just fine, but he was limited in regard to endurance. He also suffered from a condition called microcephaly, a neurodevelopmental disorder that affected his cognitive functioning. Life expectancy for individuals with microcephaly is reduced, and the prognosis for normal brain function is poor. Although most developmental milestones were not met, we were encouraged by some early progress. In the first few years of his life, he began showing progress beyond what his doctors thought possible. Like most things in life, it did not happen all at once but through a process. He developed an appetite and seemed to be enjoying food. He was mostly nonverbal until around three years of age. The good news was there was movement toward living.

What a gift it is to be accepted. It is so easily taken for granted, but it is the foundation of care and safety. We were letting Christopher know that his crooked smile and strange sounds were okay, that his broken body and damaged spirit would not hinder love and acceptance. The impact of the abuse he suffered was beginning to lose some of its power. Abuse was slowly losing out, and love was winning. His physical body would always be compromised, and this became increasingly evident as he aged. What would not stay damaged was his spirit, because all those who knew him witnessed a spirit that had been restored. He moved from surviving to thriving because of the power of unconditional love and acceptance.

Is This for Real, or Is It a Dream?

Dear Fred and Marchelle,

I was deeply saddened to hear of Zachariah's passing. I searched for a card to send, but none came close to saying what I feel in my heart for you and this precious young man. I looked up his obituary and read the many messages sent to you and your family. It is obvious he touched many lives, just as God intended for him to do. I strongly believe God sends angels to share his message of love and grace, and to teach people how to be better individuals. Only someone who was as innocent and perfect as Zachariah could do that.

I believe everything that happens in our lives is planned and ordained by God. I never dreamed I would end up working in Child Protective Services, and it was a long time before I realized that God placed me there. Looking back on those twenty-three years, I felt so blessed to have had the opportunity to see children's lives changed. So it was with Zachariah. I have often thought about that little baby I first met in a dirty trailer on Seventh Street, and how his life changed the day he was placed in your home. I knew he belonged to you and that you could give him what he needed. Through the years, when I would see you with him, I could see that he was giving you as much as you were giving him. I believe God planned it that way, long before Zachariah was born.

Fred, Marchelle, Josh, and Kristie, I don't know of any family who would have given Zachariah the life you gave him. He lived more in his twenty-two short years than many children live in a lifetime. Because of you, he had opportunities to live his life to the fullest. Most important, he knew what it was like to have faith, love, parents, family, and friends. Although I am crying as I write this letter, I am also smiling because I know Zachariah had a great life. That little baby that I first met became a prince who changed the lives of those he met. Perhaps we are the ones with "special needs," and Zachariah was sent here to take care of us.

Love in Christ,
Colleen

The decision to adopt was a process. Marchelle was the first to begin moving in that direction. There was a moment for her when she became convicted that we should adopt this wounded little boy. He had been with us only a few months, and it was during a Christmas break when I had taken Kristie and Josh on a short ski trip. Marchelle, as she often did, went to Christopher's crib and began to pray. She prayed for his physical and emotional health. She prayed he would learn to speak and connect with his world. In her prayer that night, it became clear to her that Christopher was here to stay. She knew God had given him to us, and he was here to be a part of our family. What none of us knew was that Colleen was right: he had also been sent here to take care of us.

In that moment by his crib, much began to change. Marchelle knew what was happening, and Christopher knew as well. The various home health providers caring for Christopher returned after Christmas break and began reporting that something was different. This passive and broken baby began to have an attitude. Kristie and Josh were immediately on board. They were in love with him and were quickly becoming protective and loving older siblings. A decision was being made; God was moving and I needed to catch up. I was initially resistant, believing I was too old to sign up for that kind of lifelong commitment.

My moment came on a riding lawnmower. When Christopher heard the sound of the riding lawn mower, he seemed to perk up. Marchelle would put him on the mower with me, and he seemed to be soothed by the sound and the ride. Early on, he was so unresponsive that it was difficult to know whether he was enjoying something. There was a day, a time when he held on to me as we were riding along, and I knew.

I had almost missed the moment because of fear. When the Spirit moved and confronted my fear, I knew I loved this little guy, he needed me, and I needed him. We got off the lawnmower that day, and I shared with Marchelle what I knew to be true. We both cried and rejoiced. That day, Christopher became Zachariah, a name that means "A gift from God."

Once we had committed our hearts and made the decision, we faced the uncertain journey of adoption. Parental rights had to be terminated and adoption granted. Whenever possible, there is an effort made to reunite children with their biological parents. His biological mother had never shown any interest in him, but we still needed to go through the process of terminating her parental rights. She gave some token resistance but clearly had no grounds for him returning to her care.

His biological father quickly relinquished his rights. We had never heard anything about him, but were told he had ridden his bicycle down to the courthouse and signed the papers. The social worker told us he was glad to do it and wished us well. I was grateful, but I also wondered whether he ever had thoughts about his son or questioned his decision to not be in his life. He and Zachariah's mother were never really a couple and were probably "drug buddies."

It is amazing and tragic what people are willing to avoid, deny, and compartmentalize. How did he carry this loss? Not unlike the biological mother, I believe he avoided his pain and self-medicated with alcohol and drugs. A few months after we had made the decision, we had a court date. The picture is etched in my mind of that day: Marchelle holding Zachariah. Zachariah folding into her body, safe and secure. Kristie and Josh smiling, full of joy and anticipation. We all hugged and celebrated, feeling so relieved it was finally done. Zachariah was thirteen months old the day he was adopted. I am not sure what he understood that day, but I doubt he knew its full significance. I am confident that he was beginning to know was that he was loved, protected, and cherished.

It was official. Zachariah had become a Hampton. He was starting to be more aware of his surroundings. He began to play and enjoy his toys. He had a small riding toy that he loved to get on and do circles on the patio. He was experiencing joy, he began to laugh more, and he also got angry more often—all good signs he felt secure.

Everything he did was delayed because of all his physical and intellectual challenges. He eventually started to crawl, then walk, and finally run. His gait was awkward, but he was moving. He loved to throw things; his toys and whatever else he could put his hands on. When Zachariah graduated from his crib to a small bed, he would often get up in the middle of the night. We would always hear him coming, running at full speed. He would have his sippy cup in hand as he raced toward our bed. Once he rounded the corner and entered our room, he would hurl the sippy cup toward the bed. After being hit in the head on several occasions, we learned to cover up and duck once we heard him coming.

I think back on those early months and years when Zachariah joined our family. Marchelle and I were raising these beautiful children and trying to figure out life. I was early in my career as a therapist, working at a small agency. Finances were tight, but we were getting it done. We had a small home, a car, and food on the table. Twenty-six children had come and gone. Why was Zachariah the one who stayed? Most of the other children were either returning to potentially rehabilitated parents or were leaving to live with other relatives. Our hearts had been broken by loving these children, watching them leave, and not knowing what would become of their lives. Zachariah had no one, no family, and no one to care for him. There was a good chance he would have ended up in permanent care with the state. God brought him to us, and he was ours. The truth is he was never really ours, and the reality of that became painfully clear twenty-one years later. My faith assures me our son is in heaven, and I am comforted by that belief. That assurance does not remove my grief, and neither would I expect it to.

He continued to show signs of having been impacted by the trauma he had suffered early in his life. When we were in unfamiliar places, he would sometimes hit the ground and get in a fetal position. He would begin to rock and moan in an effort to soothe himself. He was clearly suffering from PTSD, a condition often on the other side of trauma. It would break our hearts to witness how his pain and fear were being carried forward in his life. We were so encouraged when he began to welcome our protection and comfort in these kinds of moments. He was crossing over and considering that the world he had been born into was not the world he was now living in. He was beginning to utter sounds, and his broken body was healing. His spirit was open to the possibility of protection and love. His rigid body began to relax into the love that was being offered.

I have heard love is not a cure. Maybe this is true, but what we began to witness was how unconditional love breathed life into a child who had been physically, emotionally, and spiritually dying. I don't write this to garner praise; I say it as a testimony of what God was doing through all the people who were speaking into Zachariah's life. We all experienced the power of how a loving community can impact our lives. Faith was rising up, and love was beginning to win.

Zachariah was able to start kindergarten at the expected age. He was mainstreamed with some additional support through aides who would come into the classroom. He had multiple intellectual and social challenges. He had a low IQ and many physical difficulties. For the most part, other children were accepting of him, and he certainly was not a threat to them. He was passive, timid, and very compliant. I am not sure he had an aggressive bone in his body. At this young age, he was struggling with language, making it difficult for others to understand what he was attempting to communicate. He had all kinds of therapeutic resources, including speech, occupational, and physical therapies. We were pleased he was responding and developing new skills. There were many things he would do and say that were puzzling. During the period he was in grade school, he would often ask, "Is this for real, or is it a dream?" There seemed to be no rhyme or reason as to when he asked this. It was said in a very matter-of-fact way, with no evidence of any emotional disruption. We would always reassure him, and he would quickly move on to his next thought.

Maybe in those moments, he was thinking about his past and questioning the newfound security in which he was living. Zachariah did not seem to know he was different in some ways. There was no evidence that he suffered emotionally because of his intellectual and physical challenges. He did not seem to compare himself with others or want to be someone other than himself; the moment he was in seemed to be enough. The power of love and the security that results from being protected was beginning to forge some self-esteem. He was always somewhat cautious outside of our family, but within our home, he began to externalize need and desire.

He sometimes asked at odd times, "Are you my mom and dad?" It would happen when we were in a public setting or sometimes at home. It would be a very matter-of-fact question, and after our reassurance, he would seem satisfied with our answer. This was long before he had any idea about his history or adoption. As he got older, we began to share some of how he came to be in our lives. During his early adolescent years, he would sometimes tell people that his "other mother" did drugs and could not take care of him. He would also say she loved him, but because of the drugs, she could not be a good mom. We will never know about the love part. It is difficult to understand how any parent could not love his or her child. Given the fate of his mother, I shudder to think of what Zachariah would have suffered if he hadn't been removed from her care. As he got older, he said or asked less about her, and he never inquired about his biological father.

I don't know whether Colleen is right. Does everything happen for a reason? Was it preordained that Zachariah would pass away on August 26, 2014? His body was battered and broken at a very early age. There was head trauma, a stroke, and various physical challenges due to severe neglect during the early days and weeks of his life. There were multiple surgeries and many physical challenges. He took a lot of falls due to his cerebral palsy. Why did he pass away at twenty-two years of age? I have no clear answer. It is not a stretch to believe that given all his health issues, he was never going to live to old age. Perhaps even though there was such improvement and healing, a long life was not to be.

He died postsurgery after what was expected to be a relatively simple outpatient procedure. I understand all surgeries bring about some risk, but this was to be a surgery one day and eating his favorite meal and watching a movie at home the next. His fragile body had caught up with him. We had done all the prep work, taken him to his primary care doctor, and visited his pediatric cardiologist. He had the green light and was ready to go. Our lives changed the next day, and we would never be the same.

I have noticed that I don't think so much about Zachariah's death, but I give thought to his passing. I am much more comfortable with the thought of his passing. Dying seems harsh and final. The idea of his passing carries a kind of fluidity that comforts me.

Prior to his passing, I had not given a lot of thought to life after death. I had maintained a rather passive and uninformed belief in heaven. In my journey to accept this new normal, I no longer have the luxury of maintaining this passivity. It often feels that I am being required to accept what is unacceptable. To not move into acceptance would require me to separate from my life. There are times when separation has sounded like a nice reprieve. I certainly have a new understanding and empathy for the individual who chooses to self-medicate and attempts to separate oneself from the harshness of living. The truth is that I must face this loss. I know that my loss is not a problem to be solved; it is a reality that must be experienced and accepted. Anything less would not honor Zachariah's life; anything less would allow his passing to hold no meaning.

I never struggled with the *why* question. I do not believe God caused him to leave this world, and neither do I believe it was within his plan for Zachariah to suffer abuse as an infant. I do not know why God did not prevent the abuse. I do not know why God did not perform a miracle that morning when we were crying out with desperate prayers for Zachariah's life to be saved. I don't need to know; I have become okay in the not knowing. I have felt a peace that surpasses my understanding. I have been held in the assurance that this is not the end of the story. I think this is why I am more comfortable with his passing rather than his death. All we ever had was the time we had; no more, no less. That really is all any of us have. I would like to understand this better—or maybe I wouldn't. Thankfully, my acceptance of this reality is not dependent on my understanding. If this weren't true, then there would be much in my life for which I would not be able to hold a place. My understanding is limited but sufficient.

I feel fortunate that I don't curse my circumstances, but I choose to mourn them. The distinction between cursing and mourning will have much to say about how I live the rest of my life. Anger can be a healthy part of grief, and I see its value. I also know cursing can be self-centered and devoid of any risk—the risk of belief in a larger plan. My mourning is evidence that I have loved well and that Zachariah's life mattered. I also believe that if we don't value our grief, we limit what we can know about ourselves.

Most of Zachariah's life was good. He was cared for and loved by many people; more than a thousand came to pay their respects. His mother and I both spoke and thanked those who were so kind and loving in the early moments and hours following Zachariah's passing. We were so blessed when Zachariah came into our lives. He had a childlike faith that this life is not all there is. This belief is reflected in his favorite song, "Where I Belong" by Building 429, which we played at his funeral. He and his buddies had performed this song at a community talent show.

> All I know is I'm not home yet
> This is not where I belong
> Take this world and give me Jesus
> This is not where I belong

Community, We Are Not Alone

Dear Marchelle,

I am so sorry for your loss. We love Zachariah hits for him at state missing best friend great guy world Louisville Lamas missing him good memories with Zachariah. We went to Johnson Traditional Middle School Butler High School and Sun Valley. I love you so much and miss you. We miss Zachariah too so much. Meitnerium's out heart and team too so much dance with JTMS prom together, basketball together, softball together, joy prom together, lunch together, graduation together. All about Zachariah great joke on Jayden, me, Wendy, Ben, and Whitney. Or Brianna, Shelby, Matt, Roise, Tara, Hola great time with

Zachariah when saw him at Johnson Middle School. Same in class together. Marchelle, love you and miss you to be okay. Marchelle, get rest for Zachariah. Dream about him heaven, good place.

Love always,
Lauren Admas

WE RECEIVED THIS PRECIOUS LETTER SHORTLY AFTER Zachariah passed away. He had friends, he had community, and he was loved. Lauren was part of his community. They were in school together, played in Special Olympics together, and also attended some school dances together. There are gaps in my memory of the day he passed away and the funeral. One of the things I do remember is holding Lauren in my arms as she wept during the visitation. She reminded me that I was not alone and others were hurting. The depth of her sobbing compelled me to want to help her and momentarily lay aside my grief.

The special needs community is a very close and involved group of people. The parents of these children are supportive of each other and protective of their children, as well as everyone else's children. No one understands the challenges and the joys like these parents. They are bonded in their understanding of the pain, fear, and joy of raising these special people. They know about life expectancy and the fear about what happens if they die before their child. They know about the rejection, teasing, lack of understanding, stares, bathroom issues, and communication issues. They also know the joys: a child who seems to never lose his or her innocence and is forever in the moment, who at twenty-two years of age wants to hold your hand or lay his head on your shoulder, who gets you up in the middle of the night because there is a moth in his bedroom, who still needs you to hold his hand while he crosses the street. These parents are bonded in the joys and in what is hard. They love each other's children, and to some extent, they become a larger family together. They have disagreements, and feelings get hurt, but they carry on in their collective love.

Many of these children will never leave home. Some will be placed in a group home with other disabled adults. Some have family members who will pick up caring for the child after the parents are gone. There were nights I would lie awake and pray about Zachariah's care after his mom and I were gone. Both Kristie and Josh were committed to caring for him after we had passed. Call it parental ego, but I knew no one would care for him like his mother and I would. As much as he loved his brother and sister, I feared he would withdraw into himself. Would they anticipate his needs? Would they make sure his scrambled eggs had cheese in them? Would they let him win at basketball? Would they tell him how handsome he was after his head was shaved to hide the bald spot?

My worries are over; he left before us. I have a new normal. I no longer need to worry. That sort of fear has left and been replaced by a life-changing grief. Death came, and my precious son is gone. Sometimes I wonder whether it would have been easier if he passed away as an infant, or if he had lived for another ten years. Young fathers grieve the passing of a child, and so do old fathers. As an older father, I cannot imagine that my pain is any less or any more than any other father. Life is moving on. I see some of the parents of other special needs children, and I believe their worries continue. I pray for them, and I hope they are praying for me.

We are no longer a part of that community, which is another part of our loss. Marchelle spent countless hours with the disabled community. So many of these children have fragile bodies and multiple health risks. These children die prematurely at a much higher percentage due to these complexities. Like so many of these parents, we held on, trying to love in the present without thinking much about the future. We had certainly lost sight of some of the frailties of Zachariah's physical condition. It can be good to forget, knowing that to remember may have limited some of the living we did together. When I ride by the golf course he and I played on, I picture us chasing golf balls and him proudly driving the golf cart.

One of the places where this collective love shows up is Special Olympics. Cheers and encouragement are extended not only for one team but for everyone playing. The simplest of accomplishments, like running from home plate to first rather than home to third, can receive a standing ovation. Throwing a gutter ball in bowling can result in multiple voices shouting, "Way to throw that ball!" Basketball games can slow down while the child with severe cerebral palsy is given the opportunity to make a basket.

It is in these kinds of moments when all seems right with the world. In the midst of what is often perceived as something to be pitied, we held gratitude and celebration. These kinds of moments bring perspective connecting us with what really matters. Happiness and satisfaction are not measured by who is the biggest, baddest, or strongest. It is not about the prettiest, the wealthiest, or the most accomplished. These kids challenge you to not measure your life by what this world deems important. You are given the opportunity to experience the sacred. Their struggles become an opportunity to witness courage, hope, and perseverance. Simple moments, often taken for granted, are celebrated with great joy. There is nothing like an ovation that recognizes not that the ball went into the gutter but that the ball was thrown.

If Zachariah knew you, he would talk to you, but he had little to say in most of his life situations. He became more involved when he thought you might know something about what he was interested in. Zachariah had several favorite people in his life, and one was a man named Earl. Zachariah also had several obsessions, one being walkie-talkies. Earl had a history with ham radios, so for Zachariah, Earl was one of the coolest people on the planet. Earl and Martha were raising their grandson, Brandon, who was also part of the special needs community. Zachariah loved to bring his walkie-talkies to the community center and distribute them to whoever he thought might participate in some communication. Whenever Zachariah got a new pair of walkie-talkies, he couldn't wait to show them to Earl.

On one occasion, Zachariah wanted to test their talking distance. He had Earl walk away from the building until they could no longer pick up a signal. I picture this sixty-seven-year-old man walking on a hot summer day, walkie-talkie in tow, communicating until the signal was lost. On a deeper and more meaningful level, the signal really never gets lost; it simply shifts.

What happens that is good and pure is deposited in our hearts. That particular day, Earl got to experience the satisfaction of being a part of Zachariah's excitement and pleasure. I wasn't there, but Marchelle shared the story with me later that same day. I got to experience a warm feeling, knowing about a simple act of kindness. So the signal never stops; it changes. Grace is that way. It is powerful and transforming. Often it shows up in the simplest of ways. If we are not paying attention, it can be easy to miss. I carry that story with me, and it is part of what gives me hope. This simple story about walkie-talkies is deposited in my heart, and I hold it as a source of comfort and assurance that all is not lost. This and countless other memories are part of what is healing my broken heart.

The morning Zachariah passed away, Earl, Martha, and Brandon came over to our home. I met Earl on the driveway, we both cried, and I asked him, "What are we going to do?" He said he didn't know, and I told him I am not sure how to go on. It would have been difficult for either of us to answer that question. I am trying to surround my heart with walkie-talkie moments, with precious moments God has given us. I am asking God to continue to provide comfort and grace. I pray my grief moves forward and I make peace with the "I don't know," because it is a part of the fabric of my grief.

Earl and I held on to each other that morning on the driveway, and without knowing it, that is part of the answer. The answer was and is to hold on and not let go. We were holding on, but we were also being held. As important as it is to hold on, it is equally important to be held. Nothing has or will cure my broken heart. No amount of holding on or being held on to will remove my pain. What it has done is to allow my pain to be a vehicle that will transform my life. I want to continue to hold on and be held. I pray I will never know this kind of pain again. I pray because I believe this pain must stand for something, and the signal will not stop but continue. Earl could not have walked far enough for the truth of what matters to be lost. Love, kindness, and faith endures, because they have to for death to not be victorious.

There were also wonderful teachers and healthcare providers within our community who were so good to Zachariah. For the most part, other children were kind and supportive. I believe our public schools are becoming more sensitive to the needs of our special needs children. Zachariah had wonderful peer tutors who began assisting him in middle school, and some stayed with him through high school. Peer tutors are young people who come into the classroom and assist with academics and socialization. Zachariah was always enamored with whom he perceived to be the most attractive girl among his peer tutors. His favorite was a young lady named Whitney who loved and cared for our son. She was his escort to the Shine Prom, a wonderful event put on for the special-needs community. Special-needs individuals are paired with or can bring an escort for a night of music, games, and food. It is a huge event with a red carpet entrance and local dignitaries. Marchelle and I were moved to see Zachariah and others receive such wonderful attention.

There was also the occasional stare and whisper. We remained very protective because Zachariah was so vulnerable and could have been easily exploited. When he was around nine years old, he and I were passing a football in the front yard. Across the road, there was a group of older kids who began chanting, "Run, Forest, run," from the movie *Forest Gump*. I sent him in the house and went after those kids. They took off and scattered. I am not sure what I was planning to do if I caught up with them. I know that I would have measured my response, perhaps simply taking them to their parents. It's innate to be protective of our children, and it seems to be multiplied with special needs kids. They continue to be so dependent, naive, and innocent. That was part of what was so wonderful about being Zachariah's dad. He seemed to live in the moment, and within the moment was a refreshing innocence. What he enjoyed, he was passionate about. He was part of a community that didn't think twice about grabbing a walkie-talkie or putting on some police gear. No judgment, just living in the moment and doing what felt right.

Zachariah loved hanging out with his brother and sister. After graduating from college with a degree in biology, Kristie went on to get her nursing degree. In Zachariah's mind, she was the equivalent of the Mayo Clinic. With any physical concern, regardless of how big or small, he insisted we call his sister. His immediate declaration was, "Let's call Kristie; she knows everything about this kind of stuff."

He was also enamored by his big brother. When we gave Zachariah advice on a particular matter, his response would be, "Let's call my Josh." It was never simply Josh—it was always "my Josh." He had a wonderful older brother and sister. They loved him and were a crucial part of bringing him back to life. Their energy and loving attention breathed hope and love into his broken body and spirit. He rewarded them with his devotion and admiration.

He was loved by his siblings but also by his community. Zachariah grounded people and unknowingly brought them perspective. They saw his innocence and were drawn to it. He helped all of us pause, and he gave distraction from the harshness of living. He was full of hope, curiosity, and passion.

He loved really well, and all of us loved better because of what he showed us. There was a refreshing simplicity to how he lived. He was vulnerable in the way he showed up in your life, and it caused you to be defenseless as well. Pride, fear, and anger were never reasons for him to not love; they didn't prevent him from asking you to love back. Whether alone or in public, he would simply lay his head on your shoulder and tell you he loved you. Sometimes people would stare when they saw this twenty-two-year-old laying his head on mom or dad's shoulder. Fortunately, Zachariah never seemed to notice the stares. He simply kept on loving and showing his world some things about how to love. He got it; he understood in a way most of us may never know. He was free not because of having reached some higher enlightenment, but because of how easy it was for him to trust and love. This was evidence that his traumatic beginning would not have the final say. Love won, and even in his death, love will remain victorious.

Zachariah had some harsh and life-threatening moments early in his life. I am confident that once he was taken away from the horror of that life, he came into a life where there was healing and joy. He knew he was something special, that his name literally means "A gift from God." His story is woven into all our stories. Love requires us to hold each other's stories and where we find suffering to come along beside and point to the grace that offers comfort and healing. I am reminded of words from 2 Corinthians 1 and out of the book *The Relational Soul*.

> Blessed be the God and Father of our Lord Jesus Christ, the Father of mercies and God of all comfort, who comforts us in all our affliction so that we may be able to comfort those who are in any affliction, with the comfort with which we ourselves are comforted by God. For as we share abundantly in Christ's sufferings, so through Christ we share abundantly in comfort too. If we are afflicted, it is for your comfort and salvation; and if we are comforted, it is for your comfort, which you experience when you patiently endure the same sufferings that we suffer. Our hope for you is unshaken, for we know that as you share in our suffering, you will also share in our comfort. (2 Corinthians 1:3–8)
>
> So a healthy community teaches us how to hold suffering in innumerable ways. We bear one another's burdens. We share in the fellowship of suffering. We participate in this life of death and dying. This is done again and again and again and again and again. It marks us. It distinguishes us as God's people. As the community teaches us, we then are able to comfort who are in affliction. (*The Relational Soul*)

I am grateful for the love and support from a very special community. Life is moving. We made some efforts early on to stay involved, but it proved to be too painful.

Sometimes I struggle with the fact that life is moving on; it seems unfair. Other than a few exceptions, people have stopped asking about Zachariah. I know it is not because they don't care or they don't love us. I think they want us to be better, and perhaps they don't know what more to say. We were told that most of our friends would stop asking and to not interpret that as not caring. Knowing this helps, but sometimes it is still hard. For a while, when I would be in the midst of people laughing and enjoying themselves, I sometimes wanted to scream, "Do you not understand that Zachariah is not with us?" I understand that as much as our friends would like to understand our pain, they really can't. The kind of pain that comes with this loss is best understood by those who have experienced the same or similar.

Loss affects us on many levels, and we are all doing the best we can. Grace allows us to understand this in a deeper and more meaningful way. Support and love come from many different places and in varying degrees. I started seeing an old friend shortly after Zachariah passed away. He too had lost a child, with his loss occurring some twenty years prior. It was good for me to spend some time with someone who was further down the path. He knew my pain and helped me know I could be okay.

His story is different but also similar. His son had a very serious medical condition for all of his short life. His wife came up with the phrase "precious burden." I have and continue to consider my grief a precious burden. My grief is always with me, and it is both precious and a burden. It is a burden in that, if not acknowledged and respected, it can bring lies and despair. It is precious in that, when accepted, it humbles me and brings life-giving grace. It draws me nearer to God and all the things that really matter. Sometimes I experience gratitude in the midst of my suffering. The precious burden I carry has and continues to help me remove the emotional clutter I have carried for so long. What I used to hold as being so important has lost some of its value. I better recognize what is temporal, and I now have a deeper desire for what is everlasting.

My precious burden has required me to look at some things I had mostly avoided. I had not wanted to think much about how hard life can be. Once the reality of how difficult life can be could no longer be avoided, I needed to make room for the unwanted. I really do not want to live this life without my precious son. I really do not want to live the rest of my life with the memory of the morning he passed away. I really don't want to live the rest of my life with the pain my wife and I are experiencing. But I also know that to really live the rest of my life, I must create this space. I needed to and will always need to carry my grief with courage and acceptance if I am to live. Without finding a way to carry my grief, at best my life will be only about finding a way to survive.

I am reminded of Jesus's words in Matthew 11:28–30. "Come to me, all who labor and are heavy laden, and I will give you rest. Take up my yoke upon you, and learn from me, for I am gentle and lowly in heart, and you will find rest for your souls. For my yoke is easy, and my burden is light." I am comforted by these words and have experienced what it means to rest and allow God to help me carry my loss. I need to rest, and I need grace. I need the kind of comfort that allows me to hold a space for the unwanted.

The Courage to Suffer Well

> Suffering does carry an invitation. It invites us into the mystery. The mystery of suffering proves to be a profound pathway into a participatory experience with God. —Plass and Cofield, *The Relational Soul*

I WONDERED WHETHER I WOULD EVER STOP CRYING. TODAY, I am not so concerned about the question. I cried in the shower this morning as I remembered and felt the loss of my precious son. I don't cry as often, and when I cry, it doesn't last as long. It is important to never put a timetable on my grief.

Marchelle and I are both better. We have done some grief counseling and may need to do so again. Right after Zachariah passed away, we attended a three-week group called Transitions.

The group meeting was held in a church right next to the funeral home where we had Zachariah's funeral. One of the most helpful things said to me was when the facilitator asked us to look out the window at the people getting out of their cars and heading into the funeral home. He told us we were three weeks down the path, slightly ahead of those people. I remember thinking in that moment, *Maybe I can do this.*

Grief is a hard thing to measure, and attempting to control it is futile. There were and always will be people up ahead and people following. The people out in front of me are testimonies this can be done. They are a lifeline of hope and a comfort when I feel I can no longer do this journey. I've never really wanted to give up, but I certainly thought about it. In the early hours and days, I did think about suicide. Marchelle and I talked about it, and we both knew neither of us could do that to the other, and we could not do it to our children and grandchildren.

Joe Biden, former vice president of the United States, recently lost his adult son to cancer. Decades prior, he'd lost his wife and child in a car accident. Shortly after their death, he talked about his beliefs concerning suicide. He said he had always believed that only a mentally ill or weak person ends his or her life. The death of his wife and child helped him understand the kind of despair that can lead to such a horrible decision.

In my counseling practice, I have seen the generational damage done by suicide. Suicide in one generation can make that more of a consideration in future generations. What it does to the living is devastating. Suicide is born out of hopelessness and lies. I must go on; both my current and future generation need me to. I want others to know that in the depth of despair, there is hope. In my darkest hours, I do not believe God has forsaken me. I want to fight the good fight and give no ground to despair.

Early in my grief, physical movement was a part of what proved to be helpful. The first few days after Zachariah passed away, I walked and walked. I couldn't be still; frankly, I was terrified of being still. When I did become still, I was afraid the reality of my loss would overwhelm me. When I walked, I was able to feel my grief and not be so intimidated by it. I cried and prayed as I walked. Those who saw me walking probably thought I was intoxicated or suffering from some sort of mental breakdown.

Part of my walking journey was through the campus of a retirement community. Marchelle and I had been walking this path for many years, so it was quite familiar. The people I encountered there did not seem disrupted by my tears. Their faces revealed concern and care. No one ever stopped me; I sensed they understood. I concluded they had their stories; they were mostly elderly, and they likely carried losses too—maybe the same and maybe different, but still a loss of some kind. We all have suffered or will suffer. Loss is coming; suffering is on its way. If we love well, we will in all likelihood suffer that much more. Given the choice, I want to love more and love well. It requires courage to love well, and I want to be courageous.

Time has taught me that we cannot possess what we love. I have tried and failed. My efforts to do so come from a place of fear that separates me from the sacred. This effort is a saboteur of the present because its focus is on guaranteeing a tomorrow.

Fear has always been my greatest enemy. Suffering well challenges my fear because to suffer well is grounded in faith. Perhaps my suffering would be less if I had not loved so intensely. If I had held myself away and guarded my heart, it would mitigate the pain I am experiencing. This was never really an option for me, because it would have meant a marginalized life. Zachariah lived up to the meaning of his name; he was a gift from God. I knew love before I knew Zachariah. I knew the love of a wonderful spouse and two older children. And even though he is gone, love will live on. I feel a responsibility to keep on loving. I acutely understand the risk, and it's hard to imagine anything more painful than what has happened in my life. But let me share my loss with the man who has lost two children; let him tell his story to the man who has lost his entire family. Pain is relative and must not be compared.

I must continue finding the courage to love and love well. I want to love until the day I die. I have been blessed with six grandchildren. Some got to meet their uncle; some came into this world after he left it. I want to tell them about him, and I want them to witness how love can live on. Life is hard, but God is good. We are born, and at some point we die. Zachariah's death matters because he mattered. Love triumphs!

My journey in grief is transforming my life. Early on, I experienced such deep sadness, but there was also assurance that I was being held. God was comforting me as I wept. It was as if I was being held in a sacred space. Thoughts and words flowed gracefully and sometimes with an amazing power. I wanted to blame God, but somehow that did not make sense. Anger was okay, and being angry with God would also be okay. For many, that is a part of their journey through grief. It may come for me, but so far that has not been my experience. Clearly, God has not removed suffering from this world. Should I blame God that Zachariah came into a world that neglected and abused him? Not everything seems to happen for a reason. Is there a reason an entire family is killed in a car accident hit by a drunk driver? Is there a reason a young mother dies, leaving a husband

and young children behind? Good does not always win; what is right and pure is often trumped by what is wrong and evil. Children are abused; women are victimized; families are torn apart. Where is the victory in these kinds of tragedies? Evil does win some battles, but it must not and will not win the war.

When Zachariah passed away, I stood before a crowded room of family and friends at his funeral. I thanked them for being there. I thanked them for holding me in my pain and sharing some of their pain with me. I told them I was broken and humbled. I had prepared those words, but what I said next was a surprise to me. I shared that I was not defeated. I had not planned to say those words and was surprised by the power ushering them forward. I think it came from the love and support I felt from family and friends. It also came from the stirring of God's presence within my brokenness. The words flowed from my mouth with conviction and power. It was further evidence that God had not forsaken me. My pain was devastating, but I was not defeated. The loss of my son had taken my legs out from under me; I wept and screamed out in pain. The externalization of my grief was evidence that love was winning. It said that death was not the final word. Death would not suffocate this expression of love. I had lost my son, but my love for him would live on. He mattered. Death would not diminish that truth. When I cried out in anguish, love was winning. My grief was and continues to be evidence of this truth.

A few months after Zachariah passed away, I was driving into work and spotted a rainbow. It was a cold and cloudy day, and the rainbow's presence surprised me. I thought of how the rainbow was a sign for Noah that the page had turned and God was still in charge. I was comforted by that beautiful sight and the fact that even though there is so much I don't understand, God is still in charge. God is holding on to me and providing comfort and assurance in the midst of suffering. As the rainbow faded from my front windshield and began to show up in my rearview mirror, I was reminded that there is a way through and out of suffering. Hope and faith is the container that holds my suffering. We all must face our losses; we must "suffer well" in order to find healing. I am suffering, but I am not without hope. I am comforted by the assurance that through faith there is transformation, and our pain can have purpose and meaning.

I have thought a lot about what it means to suffer well. To suffer well, we must face our pain. Early in my grief, I sought out others to help me, to come alongside me. They encouraged me to face my pain and know and trust that my grief was not my enemy. I discovered in a much deeper way what is required to live faithfully. It is less intellectual and more experiential. In order to grieve and suffer well, I must surrender and expose both feeling and need. My pain—all of our pain—is such fertile ground for God to show up and do meaningful work in our lives. Understand the importance of our pain; it is not to be wasted but experienced in a context that allows for life-giving transformation. Pain has humbled me and serves as a vehicle into deeper waters. In my brokenness, I understand the power that exists within my powerlessness. "I can't, but God can" is that sweet spot where I can let go of the outcome and embrace what it means to surrender. My trust is no longer governed by what I can understand and control. It is grounded in a belief and, more important, a faith that extends beyond my human limitation. We are born with an innate ability to believe and to trust. Our suffering is the space that allows that faith to thrive.

I do not want my old life back, but I do wish I could have my son back. He was such a joy, and I loved being his dad. I would not want to give back what I have gained in my suffering. Perhaps I could not have both; maybe none of us can. What is born out of suffering can only be acquired through our suffering. What a heavy price to pay, but maybe it is the only way, the only path. I wish that this would not be true, but sometimes truth is hard and requires courage.

Right after my son passed away, in the midst of devastating

grief, I found myself in a place of supernatural comfort. The presence of God was as palpable as my grief. What I experienced was God holding me, assuring me it was going to be okay. In those first few days and weeks, I experienced a moving of what I know to be the Holy Spirit.

Today, years later, my grief continues but is evolving. I look back on those first few days after my son's passing with a strange sense of gratitude. In the midst of gut-wrenching pain so disruptive that I questioned my ability to survive, I experienced a voice from within, calling me to believe. I continue to be comforted and buffered by a belief transcending what I can understand, calling me to a deeper place. It is at this place I encounter a comfort and presence that can only be explained as the divine.

Early in my grief, God brought me resources to help me in my journey. One was a book called *A Grace Disguised: How the Soul Grows through Loss*. It is a book that is both tragic and life-giving. The author, Jerry Sittser, writes about the night he lost three generations of family: his mother, his wife, and one of his three children. He writes,

> Yet the grief I feel is sweet as well as bitter. I still have a sorrowful soul: yet I wake up every morning joyful, eager for what the new day will bring. Never have I

felt as much pain as I have in the last three years; yet never have I experienced as much pleasure in simply being alive and living an ordinary life. Never have I felt so broken; yet never have I been so whole. Never have I been so aware of my weakness and vulnerability; yet never have I been so content and felt so strong. Never has my soul been more dead; yet never has my soul been more alive. What I once considered mutually exclusive—sorrow and joy, pain and pleasure, death and life—have become parts of a greater whole. My soul has been stretched.

I love the idea of my soul being stretched. What a powerful description of what I believe is occurring in my life. The loss of my precious son has broken and humbled me. The powerlessness that exists for all of us is very real to me. I no longer hit a wall when I consider the mystery within the sacred. I am more accepting of what I don't understand, because what I am experiencing surpasses my need to understand. My intellectual arrogance has been confronted and I am finding rest. My soul has been stretched, and my desire is to fill it with what matters. I am asking God to speak into my life and fill up my soul. My broken heart is being restored, and I am beginning to hold on to grace. It is both a painful and joyful process.

There is much to be gained in my suffering, and I believe I will be better because of it. My desire is to live an ordinary life. There is such value in the simple. To simply live within my means and to want for very little. To be thankful for what I have and have it be enough. To live by the words of the apostle Paul in Philippians 4:11–15, "Not that I am speaking of being in need, for I have learned in whatever situation I am to be content. I know how to be brought low, and I know how to abound. In any and every circumstance, I have learned the secret of facing plenty and hunger, abundance and need. I can do all things through him who strengthens me."

I suffered alone during my childhood and some of my early adult life. This is what shame does to us: it isolates us in our suffering. The lie is that to externalize our suffering serves only to validate the shame we carry. Pain or suffering held in isolation is a deep, dark hole, and it is a breeding ground for addiction. In the absence of righteous grief, relief is found in what takes us away from the pain. When pain is not attended to, there will be an absence of emotional and spiritual growth. Recovery, in large part, is about our willingness to bring forward our story and experience the unfinished business in our lives. There is no shame in my grief today, and I do not run to an addiction to avoid my suffering. I am grateful I am facing my loss and seem to be moving forward.

Sometimes I have wondered whether I should be further along in my grief, but grief knows no timetable. The day Zachariah passed away, I was not sure I wanted to live, did not know if I would ever be able to work again, and was concerned my marriage would not survive. I decided I do want to live, and I believe I am a better therapist because of what has happened in the midst of my grief. My marriage is solid; it has gone to a deeper and more loving place. Grace has brought this about, and I am grateful. I cannot imagine never missing my son, and there can still be moments when this loss seems unbearable. These moments used to frighten me, but I have learned they are part of my journey. When they arrive, I hold on, I feel, I reach out, and I pray.

Much has been born out of my suffering. Out of death, there has been birth. It is acquiring a deeper and more intimate faith. I had attempted to intellectualize much of what I believed. Suffering has disrupted that kind of faith experience. Like most, I had spent a great deal of energy attempting to avoid pain and suffering. Trying to control outcomes, cushioning loss and avoiding risk, was part of my survival plan. The truth is we all are powerless over most of life. Suffering helps me understand that a good life accepts the powerlessness and creates space for that powerlessness to be transformative. It is in this space that faith is born and nourished.

The family I grew up in did not suffer well. If it was uncomfortable or painful, we simply acted as if it did not exist. I am determined to suffer well, and my desire is to have my suffering count for something. Even when my suffering hits me unexpectedly, or when I see it coming, I want to cooperate with the unavoidable and face it with courage. I am reminded again of the words from Jerry Sittser when he wrote about facing his loss.

> I discovered in that moment that I had the power to choose the direction my life would head, even if the only choice open to me, at least initially, was either to run from the loss or to face it as best I could. Since I knew the darkness was inevitable and unavoidable, I decided from that point on to walk into the darkness rather than to try and outrun it, to let my experience of loss take me on a journey wherever it would lead, and to allow myself to be transformed by my suffering rather than to think I could somehow avoid it. I chose to turn toward the pain, however falteringly, and to yield to the loss, though I had no idea at the time what that means.

Deep, meaningful love is a risky business. I love my son with a depth that is hard to describe. When we love that deeply, we expose ourselves. We expose the kind of vulnerability that puts us at risk to suffer greatly. It takes courage to love, and it certainly takes courage to suffer well. We will be hurt, and there will be loss. It requires a supernatural courage to love with a fullness of exposure to love and loss. Death will not have the final say. My suffering is not evidence of defeat; it is an honoring of the love I have for my son and the confidence I have in eternity.

Whenever I think I'm better, it never fails that I am hit by another wave of grief. At this point in my journey, I don't believe that I am ever not grieving. Even in my best moments, I am very conscious of my sadness. I often think when I am enjoying something, it would be so much better if Zachariah were here to enjoy it as well. I have been told this will fade with time. I cannot imagine there will come a time when I stop missing him. We are adjusting to a new normal. It's not a normal we ever anticipated or imagined could happen. Yet it is here, and we must face it if we are to live life.

Acceptance is a huge part of grieving. We are moving deeper and deeper into an unwanted acceptance. How do you accept the unwanted? I am still learning about acceptance. What choice do

I really have? The truth is I don't have to accept this loss. I could spend the remainder of my life bitter, or I could end my life. I have too much to live for, and the story is not finished. The acceptance of my loss keeps me out of depression and helps me grieve.

My sorrow does not contradict any of the good things in my own story. In a strange way, it is making the good things that much better. My grip on what is good has lessened because of the understanding of my powerlessness. My loss has brought such perspective in regard to the preciousness of each moment. I do not own these moments, and any effort to control them diminishes their value. Knowing these things has removed some pressure and given me a newfound freedom to enjoy. Loss and the pain that comes with it is not something to conquer. It is something to live with. If we are to live well, we must create space for our pain and allow it to transform our lives. With God's help, this is what I will do.

Everything in life is different because nothing in this world separates me from my loss. Life has sped up and slowed down at the same time. Days, weeks, and months seem to be moving much faster, and I am more focused. My prayer life is not rushed; my conversations with others are less outcome driven. The things I enjoy have a deeper meaning. I am dependent on a faith that is thoughtful and making peace with the mystery. A faith that doesn't honor the mystery lacks integrity. I don't want to simply feel better; I'd rather be grounded in a deep and intelligent faith experience. I am not opposed to landing in soft places, but I question how authentic that would be. A man I respected once told me that intellectuals tend to dry up, and charismatics tend to blow up. A productive faith is one that is thoughtful and intelligent while also allowing for the expression of feelings. The indwelling spirit of God takes up residence in both our intellect and our emotions. My understanding is helping me in my grief, and equally important, the externalization of my feelings is part of what is providing healing.

A large part of my story is filled with heartache and loss. Left alone, it is only a story of suffering and pain, but when seen as a part of a larger story, it is powerful. Without faith, my pain is meaningless and hopeless. Life is reduced to the pursuit of pleasure and the avoidance of pain. In this effort to avoid the pain, control grips the wheel. Within this paradigm, what I cannot understand has little value and should be avoided.

Believing in this larger story is not a mindless journey without intellect or inquiry. A life of faith is not about turning off the intellect but embracing what can be understood and the risk to believe in what is beyond our complete understanding. Our hearts must be open to something bigger and beyond ourselves—the willingness to risk and believe. When I fear I am losing contact with this truth, I pray. My prayers do not alleviate my suffering, but they provide a container to hold it. This container holds everything that matters and connects me with the hope that exists there. The atheist may call this a crutch; the agnostic may call it creative coping. My experience tells me it has called to me for as long as I can remember. Its call invites me into a much-needed rest and comfort. It requires nothing of me but to believe and surrender. When I allow myself to let go and lean in, I experience the grace that surpasses understanding.

    The only words that seem to make sense to me are that I am experiencing the presence of God. I will continue suffering, and because of grace, I will suffer well.

A Smooth Rock

I'VE BEEN RELUCTANT TO INCLUDE THIS ANECDOTE IN THE book. I worried that some would dismiss everything else I have written, believing I have somehow become untethered or that I am a religious fanatic. But this is a part of Zachariah's story. It wouldn't be right to leave this part of his story untold. I will let you draw your own conclusions; I am simply writing about what happened.

The morning Zachariah passed away, in the midst of all the trauma, I began making phone calls. One of those calls was to the pastor of the small church we had been attending. Pastor Pat and his wife immediately came over, supported us, and prayed for us. On his way over, Pat received a text from a woman who had once attended his church. He noticed whom it was from but did not read the message. There were many people in our home that morning, and to this day, I am not sure who all was there. Once Zachariah's body was taken out of our home, we all gathered in the living room. Pastor Pat pulled out his phone to check the text he had received. He read the text silently to himself and then asked if he could read it to all who were in the room.

> Pastor Pat, I am not sure why, but I believe God laid it on my heart to share this verse with you. "'This is the word of the Lord to Zerubbabel: not by might, nor by power, but by my spirit,' says the Lord of hosts" (Zechariah 4:6).

Coincidence? Maybe. You will need to decide for yourself. That was the most difficult morning of my life. I was broken, humbled, and terrified, and I doubted I could go on. I had neither power nor might. Something began to happen that morning and the days that followed. In the midst of devastating grief, a faith was moving, and the energy was not driven by willpower or my own strength. Something was holding me in the midst of my suffering. I have answered the question in regard to the text that morning. I invite you to consider that it is not by might or power, but it is by something much greater and life changing that feeds a hunger none of us can satisfy within ourselves.

Zachariah came, and now he is gone. I have come and at some point will be gone, and so will you. Will our stories end, or is there more to come? I believe in eternity, and I look forward to seeing Zachariah on the other side.

Prior to Zachariah's passing, I was comfortable with being comfortable. It was okay for my faith to be soft. My life had not been traumatically disrupted, so perhaps a deeper faith was not required. This familiar place of comfort is no longer sufficient, and maybe it never truly was enough. The problem with living in this space is it leaves much undefined and enables the avoidance of difficult questions. I found answers that felt good and asked little of me. I wanted to feel good and desired for everyone else to feel good. This feel-good place denied the truth in its effort toward inclusivity. A more defined faith creates space for what is hard. A more defined faith empowers me to live with more clarity and purpose.

Good stuff is often not that easy. Although I want to guard against self-righteousness, I also want to live with more courage and declaration. Faith can be and often is a breeding ground for self-righteousness. When we believe we have figured it all out, we often see the abuse of power. Truth becomes a justification for arrogance and discrimination. "I am right, and you are wrong" becomes a battle cry that promotes prejudice and ignorance.

Most of us grow up with preconceived ideas of what we will do if a given circumstance happens in our lives. Then life happens, and we discover that it is often not that simple. We put things in a box, and they refuse to stay inside. Black-and-white answers are not sufficient. A rigid faith that doesn't appreciate the mystery will have grave consequences in the storms of life. A soft faith, where little is defined, will also suffer grave consequences in the storms of life. Defining faith and living within that definition involves much more than what I feel. It moves me to what I believe and the convictions that are birthed out of this belief. A faith that has definition empowers me to confront my separateness and mortality. I believe God does some of his best work in hard places.

I think about the Israelites spending forty years in the desert. God's way can be the long way. How long will it be until my heart is no longer broken? How long will it be until I no longer lose my breath when I am confronted by my loss? There are requirements of the heart that must be found for the narrative of my life to make sense. I need to be still and let grace do its work. I want to find rest, and I want to be able to embrace the rest I find. I believe Zachariah has found peace. He has crossed over, and I too have moved from where I once was. He has moved into the heavenly realm, and we are left to find our way. My movement needs to be divinely directed in order for my loss to be livable. The Israelites questioned whether God had abandoned them. God may hide his face, but I do not believe he ever abandons us. God did not answer my prayers that morning, and he seemed hidden as I prayed. Not unlike the Israelites, I wanted God to make everything better; I wanted him to save my son. But my circumstances must not serve as a barometer of my faith. Walking this life of faith must transcend my situation and be the covering of both my sorrow and my joy.

Zachariah liked to pray. More specifically, he liked you to pray while he listened. His mom would always pray with him at bedtime. He would hold her hand and also hold on to a special rock he had collected from one of our RV trips. There would always be a list of people and circumstances he wanted to pray about. He was motivated out of his genuine concern for the people on his list, but also so that he would get more time and attention from his mom. She was not allowed to leave his side until the list had been properly prayed over. Zachariah's faith was simple, and simple faith can be very powerful. He did not seem to question what he believed, and he was confident in his belief in God.

From a very early age, he started memorizing lines from movies. Almost before he put sentences together, he would repeat lines from his favorite movies. He thought prayer time was a great time to spontaneously deliver his favorite lines from some of them. One of his favorites was the dinner scene from the movie *National Lampoon's Christmas Vacation*. When he was very young, Marchelle had laid down beside him to pray with him. In the middle of the prayer, his eyes opened, and he delivered the blessing dialogue from the movie. It was the scene at the dinner table when the elderly aunt recited the pledge instead of praying a prayer.

At twenty-two years of age, he was still leaning his head on Marchelle's shoulder, still making sure everyone got prayed for. His childlike faith kept us grounded and reminded us that it is not so much what we know but what we believe. Zachariah never hesitated when asked about his belief; it was always direct and life giving in its simplicity. There were many things that he did not know because of his intellectual challenges. He had no real grasp on theology; he simply believed. His passing has given me the opportunity to live more fully in what I believe. There are some things I know, and that is good, but what really invites the breath of what matters into my life is what I believe. I thank Zachariah for this wonderful awareness.

When he was in the sixth grade and attending vacation Bible school, the question was asked, "Who believes in

God?" Zachariah raised his hand and said, "I do." Due to his developmental delay and his intellectual challenges, I can't imagine he gave much thought to what believing was about. At some point in his late teens, he decided to start taking sermon notes. Within all the misspelling and poor sentence structure, there would often be a powerful message. At the end of each service, he would deliver these notes to Chad Lewis, one of our pastors. Chad would always thank him and affirm the message within these notes. Zachariah trusted Chad and would sometimes carry on a conversation with him. Even with his autism, once he trusted you, he could be quite talkative and engaging. He seemed to enjoy writing these notes and the attention he received from Chad. We asked Chad to speak at his funeral. Part of what Chad shared was how he had distributed these notes to other pastors, and Zachariah's notes were on the bulletin boards in several offices. These notes had touched several people's lives. His notes had no fluff, no deep theological argument. They were notes that simply acknowledged that God is love.

"He wants us to come as we are but he will see us forever he loves us like we are, and he is holy, and he knows everyone and he looks for us."

"God will get us hope and love forever and look over us and

loves one and loves one and there and God will come back one day and give us a new life and he will know what we need."

Zachariah was baptized when he was twenty years old. For some time, he had been resistant to the act of baptism because of the submersion. He loved to swim, but the thought of someone dunking him was a little too much. After witnessing multiple baptisms, he made the decision to go for it. He was baptized by Chad, who had walked him through the process and helped him feel comfortable. His mom and I helped him prepare his written testimony. His brother read it out loud as part of the baptism. Here is what it said.

> My name is Zachariah Nathaniel Hampton. It means "Chosen One" and "Gift From God." I came to my adoptive family when I was 11 months old. My birth mother had trouble with drugs and other things and was not able to take care of me. My first few months of life were difficult. I was very ill and had experienced a stroke. I was with my family for a year before I learned how to make sounds. I had to have a few surgeries on my eyes, ears, and mouth. I have a condition called microcephaly. I also have mild cerebral palsy and autism and a few other challenges. My doctors were not sure how well I would progress or be able to cope with my health issues. Then something happened to

me on the Christmas holiday when I turned two. My dad took my brother and sister and my mom stayed home with me. My family always prayed for me but on this day my mom was drawn to my crib. She felt a need to lay her hand on me and pray. She prayed for a long time for God's healing of my mind, soul, and body. She was so sure of God's presence in that room. She knew it was the Holy Spirit leading her. When my therapist returned from Christmas break, they noticed something different about me; they said I had an attitude. They said they had been waiting for that. My family knew God was at work in me. The next few years I learned to walk and talk and be in the world. My family was so proud of me.

Because my brain works different than others, I sometimes have trouble knowing what's real. I used to often ask, "Is this real or a dream?" Some things I don't know, but some things I do. I know Jesus is real. When I was in the sixth grade at Vacation Bible School, my teacher asked who wanted to become a Christian. I raised my hand and said someday I want to go to heaven and live there forever. I prayed the Lord's prayer with my family. I will keep learning to be more like Jesus. I am good at music and I can use this God-given talent to play wonderful music for others. My dad is teaching me about communion and someday I will do it by myself. I want to be baptized because Jesus was and I want everyone to know I am a Christian.

He did it; he was baptized that day. When Chad asked him if he was ready, like a warrior going into battle, he simply said, "Let's do this." We were so proud and happy. Many of our friends came to witness that special moment. They had seen a broken body and spirit come into our lives, and they were there to see the remarkable progress he had made. What a glorious day.

That was such a good day, and years later, there was a devastating day. Carrying this loss is the hardest thing I have ever done. The truth is I am not capable of carrying the enormity of my pain. If I was left to carry this alone, it would not be possible. We all must find something that provides hope and meaning. This is a critical matter of the heart. My heart has been broken. Where will I go? What will I do to rescue my heart?

Babies and Cheese Fries

ZACHARIAH LOVED CHEESE FRIES, AND HE WAS TERRIFIED of babies. Some people are afraid of clowns. Zachariah was afraid of babies. He didn't like to admit it and would get angry with us if we ever brought it up.

His fear of babies first came to our attention when he was about five years old. He was playing in one of the indoor play areas at a local fast food restaurant. He had entered a tunnel and was at the halfway point between two entrances. We were able to watch all of this because the tunnel was off the ground and made out of see-through plexiglass. As he reached the middle point of the tunnel, two babies entered, one from each end. We watched as he saw these flesh-eating babies crawl toward him.

At first he just froze, hoping they would not see him and maybe turn back toward the entrance. Once he realized this was not going to happen, he curled up and began to cry. All three sets of parents got involved as we strategized how to stop these flesh-eating babies from consuming Zachariah. When he got like this, there was no talking him through it. We tried to coach him out of the tunnel, but he would have no part of it. I suppose from his perspective, we didn't understand the life-and-death moment that he was in.

These babies were not backing up, so it required one brave parent to go in and rescue him. I knew that the fatherly thing to do was go in with no concern for my own personal safety. I decided to go in toward the baby that looked the least vicious. As I crawled past this nine-month-old who was smiling and cooing (in Zachariah's world, this was a ploy to make you think you were safe), I slowly crawled back toward the entrance while shielding Zachariah from harm. I am sure he thought we would never make it out and his mom would have to drive home alone.

Zachariah's fear of babies never really left him. Even at twenty-two years of age, he was baby avoidant. He liked his nieces and nephews but kept his distance. He loved to fix things for them and would always clean and shine their riding toys before they came for their visit during the summer. A few weeks before he passed away, we were visiting with our oldest son, our daughter-in-law, and Henley, our six-month-old grandson. Zachariah did something he had never done. When Henley grabbed his finger like most babies will do, Zachariah did not resist and simply stated, "He is such a peanut." This was a real breakthrough for a lifetime baby avoider.

It is interesting what you miss. I miss feeding Zachariah. I didn't have to literally feed him, but we bought him the food he liked. He became a very good eater. He loved certain foods, and he would occasionally see a television advertisement for a certain food and then make his request known. His requests were so few that it pleased me to see him enjoy something he had requested. After a busy week at the community center, he would often spend Saturday "grazing." He would eat and then eat some more. Eating was high on his list of what pleased him. His mother taught him a little about cooking, but mostly he used his cell phone to call up from the basement and inquire about the next food item. I miss the innocence he brought to our lives. The list is endless in regard to what I miss.

I have never been very handy in regard to fixing things. Historically, my efforts have often created more work than they have resulted in repairs. I have gotten better over the years, but I continue to desire growth in this area of my life. Men who can fix things have always impressed me. We tend to outsource so much, and I believe that it takes us away from some earthy connection. Working on projects has become a nice way for me to gain some perspective, but I know Marchelle still suffers some anxiety when she sees me with a hammer or a power tool.

Zachariah was always good about being a part of me fixing something broken. He would exercise great patience while holding a piece of something in place that I was attempting to put together. He could often see what I couldn't, and after witnessing me trying and retrying, he would suggest the obvious.

Our last project before he passed away was cutting up some firewood. I had purchased a new chainsaw, one that actually started. My previous one had spent more time in the shop than it did cutting wood. We were both decked out in our protective glasses and earbuds. After we each took turns cutting a piece of wood, we would beat our chests like proud lumberjacks.

On most Saturdays, we would visit our local army surplus store. If allowed, Zachariah could spend hours rummaging through old military gear. Most trips to the army surplus store resulted in some sort of purchase. His prized possession was a security badge attached to a leather backing with a chain he could put around his neck. He loved the thought that he was military or law enforcement.

Whenever he was in a situation when it was inappropriate to display his badge, Zachariah would simply wear it under his shirt. On those occasions, he was an undercover officer prepared to display his badge if needed. In his world, there was never a situation that did not call on his law enforcement credentials and skills. He was the security officer when his buddy Haden was Santa Claus at the community center. Zachariah would escort Santa from the car to his chair, and from the chair to the bathroom. There was no way a terrorist posing as a child would harm Santa Claus.

Zachariah was a security officer at his brother's wedding. He wore his badge under his tux. He was one of the groomsmen, and he took great pride in that. He and his buddy Haden were also in charge of seating the guests. Once a woman indicated where she would like to sit, he would extend his arm to escort her to a seat. He would fly down the aisle as if there were something chasing him. After a couple of trips, I started warning the ladies that they may get whiplash because of how quickly he took off. It was as if he had been fired out of a cannon.

Zachariah loved dressing as a law officer so much, sometimes I didn't know whether he understood that he *wasn't* a police officer. Once a week, he would participate at a facility for local adults with disabilities. Zachariah's job was to make sure all the participants knew their bus had arrived to carry them back home. He would always be wearing his police uniform, badge, handcuffs, and shoulder walkie-talkie. At home, he loved riding his three-wheel bike. We had tried him out on a two-wheel bike, but he felt much safer with three wheels on the ground. This became his police cruiser, and he was proud of his ride. He would order all kinds of flashing lights and sirens to put on his bike. After a while, it looked less like a police bike and more like a Christmas tree.

Zachariah was always taking my tools, especially my tape measure. He loved to measure whatever project he was working on, like the length of his crime-scene tape (he would play out crime scenes on the patio using caution tape) or the distance he needed to ride his three-wheel bike to dismount and fire his pellet gun at a target. I would love to be annoyed again because I'm unable to find my tools.

Springtime is so beautiful and is my favorite time of year. The warmth of the sun, the blooming flowers, and so much of God's creation beginning to come back to life. With every season, there is a reminder that Zachariah is no longer with us. In the spring, I love sitting on my covered porch, particularly during a warm spring rain. Like most things, this is met with a familiar joy and what is becoming a familiar pain. Zachariah was always in charge of lighting the torches. He took great pride in being able to do this; he both lit and extinguished the flames at the appropriate time. Putting the flames out required him to place the attached cap over the flame. His hand-eye coordination was compromised, so it was a circus act to get this accomplished. I always stayed close by in case things went south. One of my dear friends, after watching Zachariah perform this task, started calling him the Human Torch. Each time I light these torches, I am comforted and pained by this memory.

My grief has become a part of who I am. I never want to be defined by my grief, but I must accept it as a part of what now defines me. Early on, I wondered what people thought. Did they pity me? Were they afraid of me because of the pain I carried? My heart's desire is that they see a man who is working hard to be led by courage and faith. I hope that they are witness to a man who is being transformed by God. I wish that, like me, they are surprised and thankful that hope can exist in the midst of such pain. I want us all see the power of grace. Grace is everywhere, but loss and pain are also everywhere.

I've been involved with a men's group for the past twenty years. One of the men in the group recently suffered a heart attack. We know some of each other's stories and the joy and sorrow that are part of the narrative of our lives. Another good friend has just been diagnosed with cancer. The list goes on and on because of the broken world in which we live. We must not lose heart as we suffer, and we must lean into the grief that is there. We must find community and be courageous in what we bring. Others have literally and figuratively held me as I walk this journey. A dear friend from college, Ed Smith, who now lives in another state, has spent hours listening and praying with me. He too has lost a child; his was twenty-six years ago. He has traveled ahead and cleared the path to help others find their way.

There are simple acts of kindness. The woman who brought me coffee and a chair after I had spent hours greeting people at Zachariah's funeral. The server at our favorite Mexican restaurant who sat down and cried with us. These relationships, these encounters, and these acts of compassion continue to hold me up. They are evidence of the fabric of God's presence in the midst of my suffering. These things help me battle the darkness that can assault my hope. Because of all that holds me, I am moving through the darkness and finding the light.

When Marchelle and I spoke at Zachariah's funeral, I spoke about how much we all needed one another. I quoted a line from Mary Gaither's song, "Mercy Now." "We're all just walking each other home." There is only so much we can do for ourselves, and we do need each other. I have and continue to experience the compassion of others. I know their love and concern for me.

Early on, I wanted to run away, but there is no place that would have taken me out of my pain. There is no geographical cure. and any effort to avoid my suffering would provide at best temporary relief. I must accept the darkness in order to live more fully in the light. The Psalms are such a comfort in times of despair. A psalm of David has repeatedly spoken into my life and helped me accept the darkness. "Weeping may tarry for the night, but joy comes in the morning" (Psalm 30:5).

There is fluidity with my suffering where struggle tends to be static. The struggle may revisit, but the lies hold much less power because of what suffering well has done to bring truth to my life. It will be okay to struggle again if that is a part of this journey, and I am confident that suffering will find its way through the struggle. Suffering holds no lies and is pure and congruent with my loss. I do want to suffer well, and I will not and cannot do so if I don't let go to something greater. It is important to let go and trust it will be okay, particularly when I am powerless over the outcome. Life is hard, and no one is immune to loss and the pain that accompanies it. My acceptance of what is hard has helped me have a deeper relationship with what is good. I am not cured, and the truth is none of us are; we simply are better by walking forward in the context of grace.

Just a Guy

ZACHARIAH LOVED TO LEARN, AND HE LOVED THE attention he received while learning. We both enjoyed pretending we were cage fighters. I would teach him what little I knew about boxing and wrestling. He would soak it all in, and we would stage a boxing championship or ultimate cage fighting match. The blows we received were harmless; no one ever got injured. Because of his vision issues, he would typically not see my punch or movement until it was already on him. He had this way of reacting to it that would cause me to laugh hysterically. We would each attempt to get the other to tap out. Instead of tapping out, he would always pretend he had passed out. Our matches were not limited to being at home; when bored while out shopping, we would do some shadow boxing. Marchelle would always chastise us for behaving that way in public. On one occasion, we were given a lecture by what I considered to be a grumpy old lady. Zachariah loved doing guy stuff. I miss those times.

One of his greatest loves was music, and he also loved to sing. Zachariah spent hours down in the basement, singing along with the music he played on his iPad. Sometimes he got the words correct, but most of the time he made noises that sounded somewhat like the words in the song. He and I loved to sing in the car. He and Marchelle would meet me after work at a local restaurant. Zachariah would often ride home with me. Out on the expressway, with the sunroof open, we would sing at the top of our lungs. When there was a guitar or drum solo, I would say, "Take it, son," and he would mimic playing the guitar or drums. We were both rock stars, and for those few moments, he had no disabilities, and neither one of us had a care in the world.

One of our favorite songs was "Hotel California" by the Eagles. We would each take turns singing the lead while the other sang backup vocals. He was usually in key, but some of the sounds coming out of his mouth were hysterical. This was one time I would never laugh because he was very serious about music. We were both suffering from delusions of grandeur when it came to our abilities to sing. Those moments were precious, and I had an appreciation then for what was happening, but today my appreciation is tenfold. All we have are moments, and how quickly they go by. If we are fortunate, there are more moments when we laugh and have joy than when we suffer.

He had some God-given musical talent. He taught himself to play drums and did quite well. His guitar skills were lacking; he mostly pounded on the strings with the amp turned all the way up. His fine motor skills were compromised, so making a chord was quite difficult.

Zachariah had a favorite music store he loved to visit. He developed a friendship with a young man named Bobby who worked at the store. Bobby would always give him a warm welcome and was very patient and attentive. Most Sundays after church, we would stop by the music store. Zachariah would often try to get out of the car before we stopped because he would be so excited. He fell in love with a pearl white electric guitar. Each time he went into the store, Bobby would get the guitar off the rack and hook it up so Zachariah could take it for a test drive. Our plan was to put it on layaway. The week before Zachariah passed away, Marchelle caved under the pressure, and we made the purchase that day. I remember him running toward me with his new guitar in tow, saying, "Mom said I could take it home today." Bobby put some glow strings on the new guitar, and off we went. Thinking about him running for joy while holding his new guitar is a very special memory. His brother Josh now has the guitar, and I hope someday his children will play it.

About a year prior to getting the guitar, we had purchased an electric drum set from the same store. Bobby now has Zachariah's drum set. We wanted to give the things that really mattered to Zachariah to people who had really cared about him. Bobby cared about him, and Zachariah trusted him. They became friends. Bobby took the time to deliver the drum set, and he gave Zachariah a tutorial. I believe Bobby loved Zachariah, and Marchelle and I loved people who loved Zachariah. I suppose love moves in that way. It travels from heart to heart and we are the better for it. Zachariah opened up the hearts of a lot of people. We all loved better because of who he was and what he brought into our lives.

I had played the guitar in college but had not played in more than thirty years. A few months before Zachariah passed away, we were making our weekly visit to the music store. A beautiful Ibanez guitar hung on the wall. This was the beginning of my reentry into playing music. Zachariah and I would spend many hours in the basement banging away, him on the drums and me on guitar.

We formed a basement band that we called the Smoking Chickens. Each of us had a wireless microphone posted on a stand and connected to an amplifier. We pretended we were doing concerts and that we were playing at the "shack in the back summer concert series," from downtown Valley Station. We took turns introducing each other and would provide introductions for the songs we were singing. We would have intermission breaks, when we would advertise for an imagined snack bar and gift shop. We sold fried bologna sandwiches prepared by Juanita. Zachariah had collected several scarves from an Elvis Presley impersonator. We would offer them, sweaty and all, to the lovely ladies who were screaming as we played. He would get so into the performance that I am not sure if he lost sight that it was all make believe. It was not lost on me, both then and now, how deeply I love him. How many dads are able to enjoy that kind of moment with a twenty-two-year-old son? We were both rock stars with adoring fans craving our music.

Another one of our favorite songs was Willie Nelson's "Angels Flying Too Close to the Ground." I don't know whether angels inhabit the human body, but if they do, I must have been playing music with an angel. I look forward to seeing him on the other side.

Our relationship allowed him to have a little bravado, to push back in a healthy way. Together, we stepped into some masculine energy and deepened our bond. In all of his other relationships, he tended to be passive and very conflict avoidant. The trauma he carried, the physical challenges, the intellectual challenges—all of these contributed to his difficulty with standing up for himself.

I already mentioned that one of Zachariah's favorite movies was *Christmas Vacation*. We watched it during the holidays, and he would watch it at other times of the year as well. He and I loved the scene where the squirrel jumped out of the Christmas tree. He would laugh hysterically while everyone ran from the squirrel. Our favorite moment in the movie was when the entire family was huddled together in fear, waiting for someone to do something. The dad character, played by Chevy Chase, mustered up some courage and announced to his family, "I am going in," meaning he was going to confront the squirrel.

Zachariah had a real fear of moths. Yes, those tiny, flying insects that can sometimes get in your home. Whenever one would get into the house, he would panic and run to his mom or me to seek protection from the terrifying moth. On more than one occasion, a moth would find its way into his room. This would be a great opportunity to recreate the scene from the movie. He and I would huddle together right outside of his room. I would be armed with a fly swatter and would declare, "Son, I am going in." Depending on his level of fear, he would announce, "I am right behind you, Dad." It was a very simple and silly moment in our lives, yet it was a moment that warms my heart. I loved being his protector, and I love being his dad. In the end, I couldn't protect him from what parents never want to think about: their child dying.

When a child dies, when a parent outlives their children, there is a sense of failure. Those kinds of thoughts can and will do damage to my grieving. The truth is we were never going to be able to undo the physical damage that had been done to his body. Somewhere along the way, we had lost sight of how physically fragile he was. He had accomplished so much and he was thriving. Worry about the unknown would probably have limited what we exposed him to. All our adventures together served to bring richness to his life and ours. I would not change any of that because I do not believe it would have extended his life. What I do believe is that the damage done to him as an infant predisposed him to prematurely leave this world.

The reality of death and tragedy is very real to me. The distance I had kept from this can no longer be. The veil has been lifted, and I must face a harshness that is part of what is required to live within truth. My hope is not lost, but it has been challenged. I am a part of a group for which I certainly had no desire. I feel some kinship with my fellow sufferers. Pastor Chad

Lewis, lost his brother. Chad is also a songwriter. His songs have helped me find my way. Our losses are different, but I believe there is much about our pain that is similar. He wrote a beautiful song called "The Mourners."

> We are the mourners who cry out in sorrow
> We are the mourners who call out your name
> We are the mourners who long for tomorrow to not be the same, to not be the same
>
> Our voice is raw from all of our wails
> Our hands reach out toward awakening grace
> Burn some light into our growing darkness
> Give us the breath to see a new day!

We are traveling similar paths and praying for similar things. I see Chad breathing and trudging up ahead on this path called grief. Witnessing his breath gives me strength for today and hope for a new day.

I don't believe Zachariah's arrival in our lives was a coincidence. God directed him to us. Did he also decide that Zachariah would pass away on August 26, 2014? His body was battered, and his emotional and spiritual self was traumatized at a very early age. There was head trauma, a stroke, and various physical challenges due to severe neglect. He was abandoned in every way imaginable.

Once he was removed from his biological mother's home and placed in our care, there were multiple surgeries and many physical challenges. He had circulatory problems throughout his life. He took lots of falls due to his cerebral palsy.

Why did he leave when he did? "Everything happens for a reason." Those words can so easily flow out of the mouth of whoever is saying them. "God took him home." "God needed another angel." "It was his time." Words spoken easily spoken when you are not the one suffering. They're much harder when you are living in a devastating loss. Those kinds of explanations are often thrown around without much reflection. They certainly can provide comfort and assurance ... but I am not looking for what is easy; I am looking for what is true. I don't want to believe something because it makes me feel better. I certainly am not opposed to feeling better, but it must be grounded in substantive meaning. I want the fiber of my faith to be emotional and thoughtful.

I desire for God to meet me where I both think and feel. Therein lies the sacred space where my life is truly transformed. There *is* a reason in everything, and I believe that God uses the circumstances of our lives to invite us into a relationship with him. It is not a stretch to conclude, given all his challenges, that Zachariah was never going to live a long life. All he ever had was the time he had, no more and no less. That is all any of us have. I would like to understand this better ... or maybe I wouldn't. Is my acceptance of my loss dependent on my understanding? If this were true, then so much of my life would lack acceptance. My understanding is limited, and my acceptance must not be dependent on only my understanding. I know that twenty-one years of Zachariah's life were good. He was loved and cherished, and he had some great adventures. I do not know whether God chose ahead of time to take Zachariah home that particular day, but I do believe he knew he was coming, and Zachariah was welcomed with a love we cannot grasp this side of glory. After all, as the psalmist puts it, "Your eyes saw my unformed body; all the days ordained for me were written in your book before one of them came to be" (Psalm 139:16). God knew him even before he was born.

I look forward to seeing him on the other side. My faith tells me that his broken body will be healed and his words will be clear. I plan on revitalizing our band and perhaps inviting a few new members. Maybe the Smoking Chickens will be renamed the Heavily Smoking Chickens. That will be a good day, and until then, I want to live well. I want to embrace my sorrow and be fully present in my joy. I want to continue laughing, dancing, and singing. It is a decision I have to make again and again.

It is a decision that does not come easy. The kind of loss I am suffering invites hopelessness. Fear can take hold and I momentarily lose my way. Each time I have been able to find my way back to a hope grounded in faith. There is meaning in my suffering, even when I don't feel it.

When the darkness visits, I try not to be intimidated because I know it is the path to the light. The only way to the light is through the darkness. I want to run away from the darkness because of what comes with it. The truth is I can never run fast enough or far enough to escape the darkness. I must face it and make decisions about its meaning in my life. I want to be courageous and sit in the shadows, asking God to speak into my life. Faith is my vehicle through the darkness. Sitting in the darkness has humbled me. I have a better understanding and more acceptance of my powerlessness. My needs are more evident, and I have an increased willingness to expose those needs.

My life has changed and will never be the same. My ideas about happiness are evolving. I am determined to not become bitter or fatalistic. I desire to live a life of satisfaction, no longer believing in the pursuit of happiness and no longer believing that life is about being happy. I am not opposed to happiness; I am questioning its value. Experiencing satisfaction and knowing joy seem like a healthier pursuit. The pursuit of happiness can be about the denial or avoidance of the darkness. Sitting in, walking through, and allowing the darkness to be what it is provides what is required to move toward the light.

There is reward in the darkness because of the transformative power existing there. The reward of spending time in the darkness is my newfound appreciation and experience of the light. I don't take as much for granted as I once did, and I have loosened my grip on things I once thought were so important. It sometimes feels strange, but I am experiencing what I enjoy in a deeper way. Appreciating that much of what I have loved is temporal prevents me from attempting to possess what I enjoy. I am experiencing some liberation in letting go and it frees me to be more present with what I truly enjoy and love.

Much of this seems counterintuitive. As I let go, I am discovering some rest and joy that is surpassing my pursuit of happiness. I have lost some innocence, which seems strange at sixty-six years of age. I can no longer deny the reality of this broken world in which we live. My new community is the community of suffering. I feel some kinship with those who have felt or are currently feeling the impact of loss. Somehow, I am comforted by what we hold in common. It is a community I never wanted to be a part of, but I am here. It is a much larger community than I ever imagined. The truth is that this community is the community of all of us, because pain is relative and loss is not something to be compared. We are all members of this shared journey. We all have suffered, and we all will suffer. Comparison serves no good purpose; loss is hard and hurts regardless of our circumstances. Because of this reality, loss cannot be the final answer.

> God is saying in Jesus that in the end everything will be alright. Nothing can harm you permanently, no suffering is irrevocable, no loss is lasting. No defeat is more than transitory, no disappointment is conclusive. Jesus did not deny the reality of suffering, discouragement, disappointment, frustration and death: he simply stated that the kingdom of God would conquer all of these horrors, that the father's love is so prodigal that no evil could possibly resist it. (Brennan Manning, *Souvenirs of Solitude*)

These words comfort and help me hold on. My life continues for a moment, a day, a week, maybe years. I have no way of knowing. Now is all I have, and it is enough. Let me carry my loss not with hopelessness but with the hope that surpasses my human understanding.

Girlfriends

ZACHARIAH HAD A HEALTHY INTEREST IN THE OPPOSITE sex and was not too shy to speak about his desire for a girlfriend. He was awkward and had unusual ways to communicate his interest. He would do things like pretend he was sleeping when he was in the car with a female friend. We were on vacation with some friends who had a daughter with whom he was enamored. He would sit next to her in the backseat of our car, pretending he was asleep. I am sure this was a manifestation of his anxiety and autism.

One time, Zachariah and I were on a father-son camping trip, and the campground held a Saturday night dance. He was around twelve years old at the time, and he mentioned wanting to slow dance with a girl. He was so shy, and there would be no way that he would approach a girl to dance.

That night was marked by extremes. Zachariah loved to dance, and the way he danced made it clear to the observer that he had some physical challenges. I sat off to the side, just close enough if he needed me but far enough away that he felt some independence. Three adolescent boys began circling him, commenting on the way he was dancing. I moved in immediately and stared them down, and they moved away.

A young lady, who must have seen the whole thing, quickly came over and asked Zachariah if he would like to slow dance. The DJ had just started playing a slow song. I watched with tears running down my face as I witnessed my son's first slow dance. In a matter of minutes, I had witnessed both cruelty and compassion. Zachariah seemed oblivious to the taunting that had occurred, and he thoroughly enjoyed the attention from this young lady. That particular evening held both sorrow and joy, not unlike what my life holds today. That evening, I called Marchelle, and we shared in the sorrow and the joy. We cried together and held out hope that there would be future dances and that we would always be able to protect our son.

Zachariah's passivity, speech difficulty, and autism made it hard for him to make and maintain friendships. He never had a girlfriend, although in high school he sort of believed he did. There was never just one girlfriend; he typically had four relationships going on at the same time. His peer tutors would come in and assist with studies and social skills. He loved to take instructions from these young ladies. Their kindness was often interpreted as if they were interested in him. He was always polite, but truthfully, he had no idea how to be a boyfriend. We would find notes in his backpack where he would ask a young lady if she was interested in being his girlfriend. These notes would always ask for her "true feelings," such as "Do you like me for a boyfriend?" followed by a place to check yes or no. They were always kind in their response with things like "I really love you as a friend." He never seemed disappointed with their responses, and it seemed to perpetuate his belief that he had multiple relationships going on at the same time. He always had a love interest, but he seemed very content with it mostly being only in his mind.

One of our favorite weekend destinations was Nashville, Tennessee. He and I would frequent a local putt-putt golf establishment. There would almost always be a group of young people there who would be playing in front of us or behind us. They would be doing what young people do, acting silly and being flirtatious with one another. I would have moments of sadness, knowing this was unlikely to be a part of my son's life. He was probably never going to have a girlfriend, and he'd never experience the beauty and pleasure of a committed, loving, romantic relationship. Whenever I would get sad about these things, I would look over at him and see how content and accepting he looked, and I would be okay. Thankfully, the pain I was experiencing was probably projecting feelings onto him that I do not believe he was having. He lived in the moment and seemed quite happy and content.

Life has sped up, yet it has also slowed down since Zachariah's death. I am paying more attention, and I am seeing more clearly. Loss has a way of helping us come to the end of ourselves and be more present in the lives of others. For a time, there was a man who showed up outside my office building. His name was Sonny, and he was homeless. He was usually there a couple times a week. He was small in stature, his teeth were decaying, and he looked to be in very poor health. He sat at the corner of the parking lot, his grocery cart full of his possessions. He always greeted me with a smile and a wave.

After Zachariah passed away, I began to really see this man. Before, I would notice him, but I am not sure I really saw him. His smile and wave became a comfort to me. I wondered about his story. What kind of pain did he carry? What were his losses? My life was very different than his, but it began to not feel so different. What was he doing with his pain? Perhaps it was buffered by alcoholism, drug addiction, and mental illness. There were certainly moments that I wished for some sort of way out of the pain I felt. I eventually moved my counseling practice to another location. I hope Sonny is okay, and I hope he finds his way to a comfort that surpasses our human understanding.

I am grateful for these encounters, and I pray I will never lose sight of their importance. It is an unexpected and wonderful gift that moves in and out of my life. Sorrow is never far behind, reminding me of my loss and the pain continuing to be a part of my story. I want to remain courageous, not denying my pain while also embracing my joy. Both are pieces of the narrative of my life and must be accepted if I am to live a good and faithful life. Grace is allowing me to live in this story, and grace will see me through.

I am surprised I can still experience some joy. I did not think that was possible because of the kind of loss I've suffered. Sometimes I feel guilty, as if I am not supposed to feel any kind of joy. I worry that I am in some kind of trouble and am denying my grief. I am learning to enjoy the moment because I know grief is coming. The triggers for my grief are numerous: a smell, a sound, a song, a word, a look, the wind, the rain, my breath, being alive.

Most of living reminds me of my loss. Embracing my grief and accepting this journey is what I am called to do. My grief has slowed me down, and I am more aware of sacred experiences.

Two days after Zachariah passed away, on our way to pick up my daughter and her family at the airport, a man approached me at our local convenience store. I knew him, but we had not spent much time together. Marchelle knew his wife, but he and I had had limited contact over the years. When he saw me in the parking lot that day, he immediately approached me. He had tears in his eyes and spoke into my life with encouragement and compassion. He extended grace, and in that brief encounter, I felt understood and loved. He knew how Zachariah came to be with us. Shortly before our first Christmas without Zachariah, I received a letter from him.

> Dear Fred,
>
> I know that the holiday season is especially hard when you have lost a loved one. Jamie and I understand and remember you and Marchelle in our prayers. I believe it wasn't by chance that I ran into you that day at the gas station. What I said to you is what I felt that the Lord had put on my heart to tell you. Jesus Christ had a very special child of his in Zachariah, one that he had created, and one that would have many challenges in

life. It was because of this that he knew that he would need two exceptional people to be the stewards of his child, so he chose you and Marchelle to be Zachariah's parents. I feel that he instructed me to tell you, again, that he is pleased with the job you did. He would tell you, "Well done." I also think that he wants you to know that he is by no means done using you for his good works. He will allow you time to heal, but he has plans to use you and Marchelle to help many people in many ways for many years to come.

May God bless you,
Steve

I carried this letter around with me for some time. It was and will always be a source of encouragement and comfort. I don't feel very exceptional, but I do feel so blessed to have had twenty-two years with my precious son. He taught Marchelle and me so much, and he continues to teach us. Both his living and his passing have been a source of transformation in our lives. As painful as our grief is, we have gathered so many good things. Love stirs the soul and open up our hearts. Love is a glimpse into eternity. If we pay attention, love will reveal something greater than what this world will ever provide. Our hope is to enjoy the temporal while putting our hope in the eternal.

Love is not selfish; it doesn't hold on but lets go. Love understands that we can't possess; love appreciates powerlessness. Often in my life, I have settled for a temporary satisfaction because I did not have the courage to embrace the eternal. I am less afraid today, and I am living more from faith than sight. I recognize when fear is creeping back in, and I confront the lies it brings. We cannot possess love, but we can allow love to take up residency in our lives. This is a process that must be covered in grace. I want God to fill up my heart. The loss of my son and my grief can be navigated only by a relationship with God. I am a broken man in need of restoration. My heart has been exposed, and I am vulnerable. I need God to fill up my heart with mercy and grace.

Play Ball

ZACHARIAH LOVED SPORTS, AND FROM A VERY YOUNG AGE, he enjoyed tossing and hitting a ball. He seemed to never get tired of backyard basketball, practicing softball, noncontact football, and golf. His first entry into organized sports was playing on a T-ball team. Because of his vision issues and having mild cerebral palsy, he was somewhat challenged on the baseball field. I remember driving home from his first game with tears in my eyes because of how challenging it was for him to participate. Thankfully, he seemed oblivious to how different he was from other children. His favorite moment seemed to be receiving the snow cone at the end of each game. He kept playing, and we kept practicing. Over time, he got somewhat better, but he always had some limitations and challenges. His physical and intellectual challenges, along with his passive and avoidant personality, made team sports difficult.

His first attempt at organized basketball further revealed how averse he could be to anything competitive. We played a lot in the backyard, and in spite of his vision difficulties, he became a pretty good shot. When he was put into a game situation, all that changed. He would want to give the ball to his opponent rather than attempt a shot. There was no way he was going to get under the basket and attempt a rebound. Eventually, he would find his way to the foul line and fixate on looking at the people in the bleachers who were yelling and screaming. Just like with baseball, he did make some improvements. Left alone and unguarded, he would hit some shots. Even with his improvement, it never failed that after a game, he would have no idea who won. He never really learned to dribble and would carry the ball much more than he would attempt to dribble.

On the driveway, we played games like "Horse," "Around the World," and one we made up, "Whose House Is This Anyway?" The first person to make a basket would then own the court and verbally taunt the other. Once I made a basket, I would tell him things like, "Don't be coming on my court and disrespecting me." Whenever he would make a basket, then the court would belong to him. He was never much of a street talker. There would be attempts at verbally assaulting me, but he could never quite put together the words. Even in play, he had difficulty being assertive.

Zachariah showed no interest in watching sports, but he was up for playing almost any game. I have been a University of Kentucky fan all of my life, and I grew up listening with my father to the play-by-play radio broadcasts of both football and basketball games. Zachariah and I were fortunate benefactors of some great basketball and football tickets. I went because of my passion for the game; Zachariah went because of the cheerleaders, hotdogs, and pretzels. He never reacted to plays or scores of the game. He had no idea who won. He would sit and either focus on what he was eating or watch the cheerleaders.

There was one game in particular when Kentucky was playing Louisville in football. It was a close game, and we pulled it out in the last few seconds. The crowd went crazy, and people left their seats and jumped down from the wall and onto the field. In my crazed frenzy, I leaped over the wall, assuming he would follow. I clearly had lost my mind. He didn't like heights, and no way was he going to jump onto the field. Two guys ended up hoisting the nineteen-year-old man-child down, while I and two other men caught him. The entire time they were lowering him, he had a death grip on his hotdog and pretzel. Once on the field, we both ran around, hotdog and pretzel in tow.

The summer before he passed away, he was a part of a Special Olympics softball team. He loved to play softball, and he loved to play for his team, the Llamas. It was so fitting that he would be on a team called the Llamas, not the tigers or the bears. One of a llama's defenses is to spit. As I wrote earlier, Zachariah's first line of defense as a toddler was to spit. How appropriate was it for his softball team to be the fighting—or should I say, the spitting—Llamas. A week before he passed away, they won their regional tournament and were headed to state. He had played well during the regional tournament, and we were looking forward to watching them play for a state title. His team honored him by having special bracelets made, and they dedicated the rest of the season to him.

We started playing golf together when Zachariah was in his late teens. We were such a comedy of errors. He loved driving the golf cart and would often drive the ball a decent distance. We really had no idea how to play or anything about golf etiquette. Our first time out, we made the mistake of driving the golf cart onto the putting green. We watched with curiosity as the grounds keeper drove his golf cart across the field in our direction. We could see him yelling and gesturing as he approached. I am not sure what we thought, but it sure wasn't that we were doing anything wrong. When he finally got to us, we received a good tongue lashing but were allowed to continue our game.

We didn't play golf very often, but when we did, it was always a great father and son outing. It never failed that at least once, rather than hitting the ball off the tee, he would miss and then accidentally throw the club forward. Each time this happened, we would both laugh so hard that we cried. We played together a week before he passed away. We had never played better, the ball occasionally went straight, and we were able to finish the course; usually we lost all our balls and had to quit early. He never stopped enjoying playing sports, and I will never stop cherishing those memories.

On the first anniversary of his passing, I decided to go play the course we always played together. I went by myself because I needed to do this alone. I teed up the ball, grabbed the driver that Zachariah always used, and took a swing, releasing the club before it made contact with the ball. The club flew several feet forward just like it did on so many occasions when he was hitting the ball. I prayed and then cried. The truth is I sobbed.

It was good and it was hard, not unlike so many of the pieces of my grief. I teed up the ball again, and I told Zachariah this one was for him. The ball went high and far, as if God had picked it up and carried it.

I choose to believe God was with me that day, just as I believe he is with me every day. Some days it is because of what I feel, and most days it is because of what I have decided.

Killing Zombies

ZACHARIAH HAD A SUNDRY OF OBSESSIONS. HIS FIRST WAS shoes; he loved to touch, smell, and stare at shoes. Whether occupied or not, he loved shoes. He would get his face as close as possible and take in their beauty and aroma. When he was around four years of age, we were at the airport, and he got eye level with a pair of shoes whose occupant was asleep on the floor. We had to pull him away, concerned he might awaken the sleeping man.

Later in his life, he became obsessed with police officers and the military. Regardless of the occasion, he would most often be dressed as a police officer, prepared to fight a crime, or he'd be a soldier ready to take on a terrorist. Zachariah never really got older. Of course, he aged chronologically, and his body aged at an accelerated pace, but in all other ways, it was as if he was stuck in time. There were hardships associated with this reality, and there were many things about it that brought great joy. His make-believe world was fun to watch and a pleasure to be a part of. He seemed to have plans for every day of his life. His plans would often involve me engaging in some kind of make-believe activity. Somewhat like the notes he left for his girlfriends on Saturdays, I would awaken to notes on the kitchen counter that would simply name the activity, such as army, zombie killers, police, and more. There would be two boxes for each, marked yes or no. Always below the boxes would be the words "true feelings." I never got tired of these notes and the innocence they portrayed.

There were countless military battles in our backyard, and we had police training on our patio. He would ride his "police bike" to a designated spot, dismount, and shoot cans (bad guys who were holding a helpless young lady who needed rescuing) with his pellet gun. We would take turns performing this maneuver and recording our times. It always amazed me that as visually impaired as he was, he could hit the targets. Each of us would fill our backpacks with a sundry of pretend pistols, knives, and grenades. He would dress in camouflage and pack a machine gun. We would hike up the hill and position ourselves behind two trees. Our backyard became a mighty battlefield.

At some point in the battle, he would want to be captured and then interrogated. He was a fearless prisoner. During the interrogation, with my toy gun pointing toward his face, he would simply take off running. It didn't seem to matter that he had been shot at close range multiple times. He was ten feet tall and bulletproof. He seemed to believe that he was always making courageous and intelligent escapes. Occasionally, I would be captured. He would handcuff me and take me to his headquarters. Once there, he couldn't quite figure out what to say or what questions to ask. I would accuse him of crimes against humanity, and he would be speechless. I would then laugh uncontrollably, and he would follow suit. Once again, I am not sure he knew what we were laughing about.

Zombie killing was a whole different experience. We were in this together, and our lives were dependent on our skills and team effort. The most important pieces of equipment we had were his sacred walkie-talkies. He loved to charge them, test them, and shop online for them. If he could put one in your hand, you were toast. He would quickly distance himself, and you would be subject to an endless testing process. I think I might have PTSD from hearing "Testing, one, two, three." While zombie hunting, we would divide up and coordinate our positions. Our backyard was full of zombies, and thanks to his walkie-talkies and our combined courage, we were always victorious.

I had never spent much time around guns, but I wanted to honor his interest. We eventually bought one with the plans to shoot at a local gun range. He picked out a .22 caliber western-style pistol. Our first trip to the local gun range was a comedy of errors. Zachariah was in his late teens and dressed as a cowboy, and I did my best to look confident. My anxiety must have been pretty obvious because the gun range guy kept hovering around our station. I also noticed that on either side of us, they had stopped shooting and seemed to be positioning themselves to hit the ground. We were in over our heads, and we had difficulty loading the gun. Zachariah kept wanting to ask me questions while swinging the gun in my direction, and at one point I ran out onto the range to change our target without permission. Zachariah left there that day feeling like he was the man, and I left feeling relieved and a little embarrassed. I should have enrolled both of us in a gun safety course before setting foot on the gun range. Nobody got shot, and I look back on that day with gratitude and a chuckle. We loved the adventures, and the truth is some days the most important thing you can do is go out and kill some zombies.

I started doing some camping when my oldest son, Joshua, became a Boy Scout. The truth is I reluctantly started camping. My family camped when I was growing up. Our camping trips were typically characterized by everyone getting sunburned, and my parents drinking too much and getting into verbal fights. As a young man, the thought of camping had no appeal. Wanting to be a good dad meant I needed to suck it up and go camping. To my surprise, nobody got drunk, and it was mostly enjoyable. That was the beginning of decades of outdoor adventure. We bought a tent, and then we bought a pop-up. Then we bought a travel trailer, and then we bought a class C (truck with a box on the back), then a class A (looks like a big bus), and finally the mother lode: a class A with a diesel engine. I was hooked. It was kind of like what they say about tattoos: nobody gets just one.

The older two kids went off to college, marriage, and careers. Marchelle, Zachariah, and I traveled the country. Our RV was aptly named *Zachariah's Adventure*. We were living some of our dreams. We vacationed on the beach, traveled throughout the West, and did weekend trips in our home state. There was truly a sense of freedom when we hit the open road. We would drive all day and then find the local Walmart and spend the evening camped out in their parking lot. Once we left home and headed west, I would don my cowboy hat (Zachariah already had his own), and I was no longer Fred the nerdy therapist. I was a 5'8" (that's probably a stretch) chiseled man, full of what every man wanted to be and what every woman desired. We would hit the open road, Marchelle and I typically up front, and Zachariah at the dining table enjoying music or a video.

I purchased my cowboy hat in Williams, Arizona. It is hard to be in Williams and not take on the cowboy persona. Zachariah helped me pick it out. He was already decked out in his hat, cowboy shirt with sheriff badge, cowboy boots, and gun belt that he had purchased in Williams. We both loved being out west and would take on the look and feel of being a cowboy. We all took cowboy names: he was Slim, I was Buck, and Marchelle was Prairie Flower. Marchelle was never crazy about her assigned name but tolerated our transformation.

We had some great adventures. We rode horses in South Dakota, Zachariah drove a team of mules in Montana, and we did some river rafting in Wyoming. We were passengers on a train at the Grand Canyon, where there was a reenactment of a train robbery (I'm not sure whether he knew it wasn't for real). We hiked the Grand Canyon, and he commented, "Are we done looking at big rocks?" All this and more serve as precious memories that feed my soul and remind me of our life together, particularly that it was good. With time, I am able to think back and both cry and smile. I am grateful for what we shared. These moments, followed by other moments, connect me to what matters.

What matters? I have always been a reflective person, and at times I can get wrapped around trying to answer the unanswerable questions. I am more peaceful today with the mystery. The unanswered questions no longer threaten my faith. The comfort and assurance my faith has afforded me has transcended some of my need for answers. My grief continues to bring me to new places that offer new awareness. I want my grief to stand alone because when it stands alone, it is pure and life giving. The substance of my grief is love, because love is not just what feels good; it can also be what hurts. That's why love is not for the faint of heart. It takes courage to love, and it certainly takes courage to grieve.

Lies try to come in and assault grief. These lies are packaged in fear, guilt, and shame. They tell me that life is over, that I will never be okay, and that I could have saved my son. They try to convince me that nothing matters. I recognize now when they show up, and I understand this is the place where war is waged. This is the place I must fight the good fight; there is a righteous battle to be fought. I am acutely aware there is good, but there is also evil. Sometimes the attack is full on, but more often it is subtle and insidious. I must stay aware and be intentional in relationship to my grief. The truth really will set us free, and I am convicted about living in the truth.

I have learned quite a bit from the people I have counseled. Those who are immersed in the twelve-step tradition talk about finally living life on life's terms. In other words, they are living in truth, facing the hard stuff, and walking through it. This is the journey that molds and forms our characters. My suffering is that space where fears encounter truth and life is transformed.

Walk and Talk

"WALK AND TALK." MARCHELLE AND I MUST HAVE SAID THIS to Zachariah a thousand times. It was hard to keep him moving. When he wanted to tell you something, he would be painfully slow. I witnessed many of his friends, and even some adults, move away from him in midsentence because it was taking him so long to articulate his thoughts. He loved to describe in detail what he was interested in. Walkie-talkies, music, guns, military, and the police were his favorite topics. If he could get you cornered, you were going to be a captive audience for awhile. Whenever we were in a time crunch, it was a challenge to get him ready and out the door. It seemed that all his thoughts required stopping in our tracks so he could provide details of what he needed to say. Hence, "Walk and talk" became quite a mantra in our home. He made some progress, but his preferable way of communicating was clearly motionless and obsessive. He could get on a topic and camp out there for as long as he had an audience.

Shopping on the internet became a manifestation of his obsessiveness. If allowed, Zachariah would spend hours researching things like military flashlights and flashing lights for his three-wheel bike. When he found the perfect flashlight, he would seek out our approval and would try to sell it by telling us, "This is so sweet."

I miss the "walk and talk." There is so much I miss. I miss the sound of his voice, his smell, and hugging his skinny body. Marchelle slept with one of his T-shirts under her pillow for months, trying to hold on to some semblance of his presence. Holding on while letting go has been a journey of both contradiction and confusion. Like so much of life, it has and will always be a process.

Zachariah's Schedule

10:00 a.m.—wake up
Go to the bathroom
Wash hands
Breakfast
Clean room

Get dressed and ready for the day (brush teeth, mouthwash, and deodorant)

Enjoy the day's activities (look on refrigerator)

Lunch

Music

Read or cook

Community life support

Run errands

Special activities

Dinner

9:30 p.m.—Shower, wash hair, and body

Dry off!

Put on deodorant and body spray

Get dressed for bed, brush teeth, and comb hair

Help him shave, apply face lotion

Lay out clothes for the next day

Watch a movie?

In bed by 11:30 p.m., which means prompting him at 11:00

He needs 11–12 hours of sleep each night

These instructions were posted on the back of his bedroom door. He was never an oppositional child; he simply had difficulty staying focused. Being his parent was labor intensive, and it was also a labor of love. He required a great deal of instruction and direction. We could not simply send him to his room to clean because he would get distracted and overwhelmed. Patience and hands-on involvement were always required to get a task done. This was never going to change. Marchelle and I did a pretty good job of tag teaming. He never really paid much attention to this list on the door. He simply got up and enjoyed his day. Instructions were good and provided some structure and organization, but they were never going to cause Zachariah to be more disciplined in doing his chores. We accepted this reality and knew how important it was for us to not expect what he couldn't deliver. We would often make chores a game, and he and I would end up in a wrestling match on the floor.

He enjoyed the show *Cops* and loved it when I would act out a takedown scene as if he was being arrested. I would yell, "On the ground now," and force him to lie down on his stomach while putting him in handcuffs. He would provide some resistance as if he was attempting to escape. I would ask him if he had anything sharp in his pockets such as a crack pipe or a knife while I patted him down. He loved this sort of thing and would be swept up in the moment. He owned as many handcuffs as he did walkie-talkies, so there was never an issue having quick access to either. Once I got him on his feet, we would go to the make-believe courtroom, where I quickly became the prosecuting attorney. I would grill him with questions for which he had no answers. He then would quickly bolt, and the whole process would start over. We played this game when he was ten, and we were still playing it when he was twenty-two years old.

His body was failing him, but his innocence continued on. He was always giving me a better perspective. Every day was a good day for Zachariah, because he had no worries. He was so generous, affectionate, and forgiving.

Money, specifically the counting and understanding of how much to give the cashier and what change to expect back, was always challenging for Zachariah. If you offered him a ten-dollar bill or five one-dollar bills, he always chose the latter. He believed more bills in his hand meant that he had more money. While on vacation, we always gave him a certain amount of money for souvenirs. He loved carrying the money around in his billfold and making his own purchases. Once he was at the counter making his purchase, he would typically tell the cashier that he was rich and then pull out his money. Regardless of the price, he would always want to give all the money he had toward his purchase. I loved watching the whole event unfold. Most of the time, people were patient and seemed to enjoy the very innocent moment.

His lack of understanding and appreciation of money also meant he did not understand when he had spent it all. Even at twenty years old, he was like a small child who believed his wallet was supposed to simply fill back up. Zachariah believed that most things were supposed to fill back up.

In spite of all the hurt he had suffered early in his life, he seemed to have no concept of evil. Good guys always won in Zachariah's world. Goodness always filled in and replaced the bad stuff. If he trusted you, he *really* trusted you. He taught me so much; love and faith came easy for Zachariah because he had very few questions. He kept it simple and trusted in what was good. Disappointment and hurt were quickly covered with hope and love. He knew how to love because he was not hindered by fear or pride. The freedom he loved with was such a testimony to the power of his innocence and trust. Zachariah had faith in love, had unknowingly confronted what had abused him, and gave it no power in his life. His trust and willingness to love spoke a clear message to the abuse he had suffered. He was right about the good guys winning. The lies that were born out of abuse held no ground in his life. He was, and is, a testimony to the power of grace. This grace filled up the spaces in his heart where hurt and shame once lived.

Zachariah was well into high school before he stopped having bathroom issues. It was not unusual for Marchelle and

I to get a call requesting that we bring a fresh set clothes for him to change into. We would clean him up and send him back into his class. As he got older, I became the primary caretaker in this area, believing it might be more comfortable with his dad doing the cleanup duty. He never seemed embarrassed or concerned about what his classmates might think. I would get him cleaned up, and he would march back into class as if nothing had happened. His ability to control and predict bowel movements was certainly compromised. Some of this was physiological, and some was his lack of communicating need. We worked on him giving his teachers some sort of signal that he needed to go to the bathroom. He would do fine in rehearsals at home but struggled with real life situations. All of this was a reminder of how passive he could be. Outside of his relationship with his mom and me, he had such difficulty asking for what he needed. This served to make us that much more protective.

Zachariah never seemed to be afraid of scary movies. He loved to watch them with his brother and would brag about how he was not scared. His favorites were the Goosebumps movies. I am not sure whether those stories would legitimately classify as scary, but he thought he was big stuff for not being afraid. Occasionally, he and I would watch something a little more frightening. During the scarier part of the movie, I would often have my hands covering my eyes, peering at the TV through the cracks in my fingers. Zachariah would be watching with eyes wide open, never budging or reacting.

Zachariah loved the nighttime. He loved to stay up late, pulling out his toys and gadgets. As he got older, he loved to rearrange the lights and horns on his three-wheel bike. He would stretch out as much crime scene tape as possible throughout the garage. He would then turn off the lights in the garage and turn on all the lights and the sirens on his bike. We would awaken to the sounds blaring from the garage. I would typically find him in full police gear, sitting on the bike and waiting to bring justice to the world. The scene would be so hilarious that it was difficult to be upset about being woken in the middle of the night.

In the early days after Zachariah passed away, I was afraid to go to sleep for fear of the reality I knew I would wake up too. Anxiety and fear were ever present and threatened to disrupt my grief. It was difficult and continues to be difficult to find God in the darkness, but I trust that he is there. "Don't be afraid of the darkness" became a battle cry in the midst of my grief. I knew I needed to take my hands away from my eyes and expose all I could see and feel to the reality of my loss. Walking in the darkness involved the acceptance of my anxiety and fear. This anxiety and fear is not evidence that God has forsaken me; it is a reminder that I am not home yet.

I'm adjusting to a new normal. Our loss has mandated a recalibrating of our lives, and with it has come a mixture of very difficult and very wonderful things. I continue to be amazed and thankful that I can use the word *wonderful* as a partial description of my journey. It is a different kind of wonderful. My new wonderful does not contain some of the temporal feelings that once were there. My highs are not quite as high, and my lows are not quite so low. I no longer pursue happiness because of my understanding of its limitations. My desire is to live a satisfying life that will have its joys but will also contain its sorrows. Through God's grace, I will make peace with the hardships of life and bring new perspective to what it means to live well.

When Zachariah used to ask, "Is this for real, or it is just a dream?" it showed his difficulty with separating the real from the unreal. It was symptomatic of the necessary disassociation often needed to survive trauma. Recovery and healing involves the integration of that trauma into one's life so that it no longer holds the fear and disruption it once did. Early on after his passing, I had moments where I echoed Zachariah's question:

"Is this real, or is this a dream?" If we are to do more than survive on the other side of trauma, we must face the unwanted reality. To truly live, I could not attempt to deny what was true, regardless of its horror. The integration of this trauma into my life was absolutely necessary if I was to live beyond it. What I experienced could either serve to stop me from living or provide a deeper reason to live with more courage and love. I chose the latter, or maybe the latter chose me; I am not sure. When I thought about it then, and when I think about it now, I am not sure why I pressed on.

I know I can no longer deny the brokenness of the world we live in. There is also goodness in this world, and I want to breathe in everything that is pure and life-giving. I want to finish well and to do this, I must suffer well. I lived in too much fear for far too long. I told Zachariah the day before he passed away that I believed he was a warrior. He always loved when I characterized him as strong and courageous. I want to be a warrior for the rest of my life—a warrior who is full of powerful and life-giving grace.

There is a freedom within grief and suffering. My grief has removed barriers and confronted fear. It is proving a freedom that liberates me from the constraints of fear and lies I have carried. I am invited into a holiness that liberates me from the shackles of this world. My grief is part of my warrior nature because the tears are evidence of courage and acknowledgment of what matters. We are headed home, and the acceptance of the unwanted is a part of what both lies behind and is waiting ahead. We need not fear because grace will see us through.

Maybe the Ending Is the Beginning

> There is a time when you believe everything is finished. That will be the beginning. —Louis L'Amour

"LET'S ASK THE BIG FELLA." WHENEVER ZACHARIAH DISAGREED with a decision his mother made, he would often utter those words. It would always defuse whatever tension that was occurring in the moment. Often, I'd have no idea what was going on and would typically say or do the wrong thing.

He was always making us laugh, and I miss those wonderful and funny moments. When he passed away, I wasn't sure whether I would ever laugh again. Laughter has slowly found its way back into my life. My sense of humor has also returned, and I am grateful.

It has been five years since he left this world. There is much I am grateful for, and it surprises me that I carry gratitude in the midst of such grief. It seems contradictory, but the truth is that life must hold a space for both gratitude and grief. A good life requires the willingness and faith to hold each. I never felt much like a "big fella," but my grief has required things of me that probably fit under that category. It requires courage to grieve, and although I haven't felt very courageous, I am confident that courage and faith have empowered my journey. It is a different kind of courage, and it certainly is not about bravado. The courage within my grief is a place filled with mercy. The road has been narrow, with so many invitations into the abyss. Suffering was never removed, but a way to suffer was gifted. In my darkest moments, I sensed a voice calling me forward. It reminds me of a wonderful story by an unknown author.

> There were two horses in a field. From a distance, each horse looks like any other horse. But if you get a closer look, you will notice something quite interesting. One of the horses is blind. His owner has chosen not to have him put down but has made him a safe and comfortable barn to live in. This alone is pretty amazing. But if you stand nearby and listen, you will hear the sound of a bell. It is coming from a smaller horse in the field.

Attached to the horse's halter is a small copper bell. It lets the blind horse know where the other horse is, so he can follow. As you stand and watch these two friends, you'll see that the horse with the bell is always checking on the blind horse, and the blind horse will listen for the bell and then slowly walk to where the other horse is, trusting he will not be led astray. When the horse with the bell returns to the shelter of the barn each evening, he will stop occasionally to look back, making sure that the blind friend isn't too far behind to hear the bell.

Like the owners of the two horses, God doesn't throw us away just because we are not perfect, or because we struggle and have challenges. He watches over us and even brings others into our lives to help us when we are in need. Sometimes we are like the blind horse, being guided by the little ringing bell of those whom God places in our lives. At other times, we are like the guide horse, helping others find their way. Good friends are like that. You may not always see them, but you know they are there. Please listen for my bell, and I will listen for yours.

At times I have been blinded by the enormity of the loss I am living with, yet I walk on toward a hope for tomorrow.

Despair has clouded my vision at times. The darkness within my pain can catch my breath. I am so grateful for the sounds that call me out of the darkness. The comfort of someone who loves me, the testimony from someone that is further down the path, the sounds of my grandchildren, the shared history with a woman who loves me—all this and more serves as an invitation to continue on. I walk toward what is healing and life giving. I'm doing better at looking back, knowing there is probably someone behind me who needs to hear my voice testifying that we can walk out of the darkness.

I am reminded of the words of Jesus: "Come to me, all who labor and are heavy laden, and I will give you rest. Take my yoke upon you, and learn from me, for I am gentle and lowly in heart, and you will find rest for your souls. For my yoke is easy, and my burden is light."
(Mathew 11, 28-30)

Sometimes I question why Marchelle and I have been able to do the things we thought we would never be able to do. I wasn't sure whether I could work again, have fun again, and love again. A friend asked me if I could see her friend who had lost her twenty-two-year-old son from a drug overdose. On the day he died, she stopped participating in life. Some days she won't leave the house, and she will spend the entire day in her son's bed. I wondered why I seem to be living life, and this woman seems to have given up. I don't believe I am that different from her. Perhaps her circumstances make it much harder to believe and move forward.

I am not sure how much of where I am is because of a decision I have made, but there must be some active decision that is a part of helping me carry this heavy load. It would seem I have no real choice in the matter, yet there are choices to be made. Within my suffering and because of my suffering, I am experiencing a freedom like no other. All of the artificial buffers and supports have been crushed by the loss of Zachariah. The awareness of my powerlessness is so acute that I am living with a much greater dependence on the source of my hope and purpose. A good life is one that is deeply generous, knows how to rest, and is increasingly dependent on God. My desire is to live this way, and doing so requires me to get out of my own way.

There is a movement within my grief that I can only understand as the presence of God. In my darkest days, I have not lost all hope. I have not been able to blame God. Prior to Zachariah's passing, I struggled some with unbelief, and I am the kind of person who can overthink almost anything. My prayers were not answered the morning he passed away. As the EMTs performed CPR, we pleaded with God to save our son. That did not happen, yet my faith has been strengthened in spite of the unanswered prayer.

Life continues for now, and I am carrying with me this enormous loss. This loss continues to be unwelcome and unwanted, yet it is with me. Faith holds a place for this loss, and with faith brings hope. Sadness and joy seem like strange bedfellows, but I am living evidence that they can coexist. My sadness seldom disrupts or contradicts my joy. It is an ever-present reminder of my loss and the suffering in life. My sadness brings perspective to my joy, which helps me appreciate joy in a much deeper and more meaningful way. Suffering is requiring a dependence on grace. The deeper dependency is inviting me into the sacred, the place where sadness and joy do not disrupt or contradict. To live honestly and with integrity, I must hold a space for both sadness and joy.

I sometimes wonder what will be the rest of the story. The narrative of my life, the narrative I had written in my mind, has been painfully disrupted. For now, my life is continuing, and I am finding ways to live within the changes that have occurred. Since Zachariah's passing, I have become more aware of the joy and the pain that this life brings. All our lives, we will encounter both, and we must find acceptance of both if we are to truly live.

> Midway along the journey of our life
> I woke to find myself in a dark wood,
> for I had wandered off from the straight path.
>
> How hard it is to tell what it was like,
> this wood of wilderness, savage and stubborn
> (the thought of it brings back all my old fears),
> a bitter place! Death could scarce be bitterer.
> But if I would show the good that came of it
> I must talk about things other than the good.
> —Dante

Sometimes the only way to the good is through the hard. Sometimes the beginning starts at the ending. Sometimes what looks like the end is merely a pause in the narrative of the story.

We almost didn't adopt Zachariah. When he first came to live with us as a foster child and stayed a few months, he gained some weight and strength and left our home to be with a relative. We assumed this would be the end of our time with this fragile and broken little boy. He would be like all the others we had cared for, staying with us before being placed in his forever family. But sometimes the end is only the beginning.

This season in my life has felt like an ending, but the truth is it is not finished. Zachariah lives on, and he lives in many places. He lives in glory, and he also lives in the lives of all the people he has touched. Everyone who met him has a Zachariah story; he made people laugh and brought wonderful perspective to all of our lives. People wanted to be around him because he told you what mattered not so much through what he said but through the innocence with which he lived. He was a young man who had been neglected and abused to the point of near death. He had no bitterness and no fear; he trusted and he loved. Unknowingly, he broke down your defenses and opened your heart. It was easy to trust him because there was no pretense, no ego. I miss him so much, and I will miss him for the rest of my life.

Last Things

IT CAN BE DIFFICULT FOR ME TO SEPARATE AVOIDANCE OF grief from a healthy decision to situationally compartmentalize my grief. Whenever I see a picture of us together, I can quickly be in disbelief with the enormity of my loss. I can choose not to think about it and move on through my day, but is that what is most healthy? Living with trauma is hard and complicated. There continues to be times that the grief comes without much thought, and I try to embrace it and not be intimidated. I continue to have moments when I need to pour out my suffering. When it comes, it is like a river emptying into the sea. I am struck with such helplessness and fear that claim life is over and there will be no more joy. So far, grace has arrived in those moments and confronted the lies. I find my source, or my source finds me, and I am comforted and assured that the story, my story, is not done.

I don't want to think about the day he left this world, but I must in order to stay true to the narrative of his life and my life. My memories are mixed with gratitude and disbelief. I am so thankful for the life we had together, and I am so devastated that he is gone. It is difficult to think about the week and the day of his passing. There were many last things, and I want to hold them all with courage and faith. My connection with him lies in the memory of him. My friend, who lost his daughter twenty-six years ago, tells me that there are days, weeks, and sometimes months that go by that he does not think about her. I can't imagine going a day without thinking of Zachariah.

Our local community church invited him to sing special music as a way to introduce the special-needs ministry they were starting. He not only sang, but he also took the opportunity to preach. It was difficult to make out all the words he was singing, but there was no doubt about his passion and stage presence. These kinds of moments would always move me to tears, knowing how far he had come. Often, when he would leave the stage, his stage persona would quickly disappear, and he would become withdrawn and quiet. People would approach him with praise and appreciation. We would coach him to be more responsive with little success. I like to think he had a large measure of humility, but I think the truth is that his autism took over.

Our last horse ride together was very special. The summer before he passed away, we took an RV trip to the battle site of Custer's Last Stand in Montana, and then we went on to Yellowstone and the Grand Tetons. Zachariah had been on several horseback rides over the course of his twenty-two years. He was comfortable on a horse as long as there was only walking and no trotting. This particular ride was special because of the beauty of the Tetons. The day was rainy, and we thought our ride would be canceled. The ride was on, and we were issued a cowboy slicker (a full-length yellow raincoat). Zachariah was decked out in his jeans, cowboy shirt, cowboy hat, boots, holster, and toy gun. He looked the part of a real cowboy. We sat at a picnic table with one of the outfitters while the other outfitter saddled our horses. While we were at the picnic table, the outfitter gave us basic instructions. We had already given them a heads-up that there would be a young man with special needs on the ride. Zachariah was visibly nervous and began to shake. When he was nervous, he could be quite talkative, so he began to ask all kinds of questions. The outfitter was patient and reassuring.

We mounted our horses and headed out toward the mountains. The rain gently poured from the sky as we rounded a lake on our way to the edge of the mountain. My horse was directly behind the horse Zachariah rode. I could hear him talking to his horse and calling him by name. I remember feeling so proud of him that day and loving the fact that he was, for that moment, living as a cowboy. He was a cowboy, six feet tall with no disabilities, prepared to herd cattle and run the bad guys out of town. It was one of so many moments I witnessed that showed what really matters. He was always reminding me that all we have is today and that I should keep it simple. He got off his horse that day full of himself and anxious to tell his mother about the adventure.

We attended a dinner party the week before he passed away. He decided that he would like to inform the dinner party of his upcoming surgery. Our host kindly announced that Zachariah needed a moment to share something. He stood up and, with a great deal of poise, talked about his upcoming surgery and the specifics of how it would improve his vision. I was so proud of him that evening while also feeling incredibly protective. Although Zachariah could be very shy and withdrawn, he was not that way in front of an audience. All the time he spent in the basement playing and singing music seemed to prepare him for the stage.

The last haircut. There were many lasts, but of course, I had no idea that they would be some of the last things we did together. Zachariah, at around eighteen, began to experience premature baldness. He would sometimes comment about it after looking in the mirror, but for the most part, it didn't seem to matter. The week before he passed away, we had decided to do what many people call a staycation, or a vacation at home; we did not leave the city and did fun things close to home. He and I decided to play some golf in the afternoon and get him a haircut. I remember that day, looking at him sitting in the barber's chair; he looked like this man-child. He was physically aging at what seemed to be at an accelerated rate while also remaining so innocent. I felt so protective of him that day, and I was appreciative of how trusting and undefended he was. He was sitting in the barber chair, and his hair was cut short enough so his bald spot would not be so obvious. He was not concerned or vain; he was focused on how soon we could get to the golf course. Like always, he got some stares while at the barber shop.

We played golf that day, and it would be the last time we played together. Neither one of us knew how to play; we had been playing for a relatively short amount of time. That last day of golf was the best golf we had ever played. The ball occasionally went straight, and we didn't lose all our golf balls before the ninth hole. Both of us would beat our chests after what we considered to be a good shot from the tee. He drove the golf cart, and I enjoyed the ride. We were a great team, and it was a great day. Life was good, and he couldn't wait to get home and tell his mom how well he'd hit the ball.

I don't think any of us knew what he knew. Each day was a new day, and every day he loved, he really loved. He loved in such a way that it helped others love. Without knowing it, he disarmed you and invited you to show up. He broke down barriers of fear and anger. His presence, if you were paying attention, calmed you and helped you be more present. He was always reminding me how important it is to pause, to breathe.

That week was filled with simple and fun activities. We went to a minor league baseball game, ate sushi at his favorite restaurant, swam, watched movies, and of course killed some zombies. We watched some guy movies down in the man cave. Each of us would carry our unloaded pistols downstairs and pretend that we needed them for battle. He always fell asleep in the chair while maintaining a tight grip on his pistol. It was a good week, and I am so grateful we had that time together.

There are so many wonderful memories: vacations we took, sports we played, movies we watched, restaurants we loved, parties, and weddings. Zachariah loved to dress up. He was the ring bearer in his sister's wedding and a groomsman in his brother's. During the reception party, we cleared the dance floor so he could dance to Michael Jackson's "Thriller." I hold onto those precious memories while I am letting go of Zachariah.

Letting go is hard, but it is necessary if I am to live a life of faith. During my daughter's wedding, the wedding party needed to move from the back of the church to the front entrance. It was a beautiful winter day, the air was crisp, and there was a light snow falling. As we walked along the side of the church, I heard the four-year-old flower girl say to her dad, "Daddy, pick me up and don't let me go." I had to catch my breath in that moment, knowing I was about to let my little girl go. I've needed to catch my breath a lot in the time since my precious son left this world.

Holding on to things is what our human condition encourages. We seek comfort and security in what we can hold on to. Often, the source of all our anxieties and our depression flows from our efforts to hold on. I must let go of what I have lost and continue to let go of all the things I can lose. Paradoxically, I then hold onto the source that returns me to what I love. My relationships are changing because I am no longer clinging to what I am powerless over. I am beginning to live and love in a context of surrender. As John Eldredge from Ransomed Heart Ministries said, as long as our joy and satisfaction is tied to what we can lose, we are vulnerable. What we must surrender to is that which we cannot lose. When we discover the source, it becomes both the anchor and the shining light at the end of the tunnel.

The last thing, the last earthly thing. It has been so hard to think about the last day, the day he passed away. The last day is full of trauma. I know this day must be faced and covered with grace. There are many things I remember about that day, but there are also huge gaps. For grace to cover that day, I must face my fear. The trauma of that day holds some fear, and when I consider that day, there can be a physical reaction.

Prior to Zachariah arriving in our lives, he had suffered a stroke. This resulted in some facial deformity and compromised vision. The drooping in one of his eyes occluded his vision. We were encouraged to have this attended to through surgery because of the probability of further deterioration of his vision. I remember the wait. Marchelle and I went down to the coffee shop and walked outside the hospital building in a small park, finding a farmers market adjacent to the hospital cafeteria. His physician informed us all had gone well, and we would be in post-op shortly. We arrived in post-op and saw how much difficulty he was having waking up from the anesthesia. He was thrashing and confused and very agitated. Marchelle and I, along with the nurse, worked to calm him down and help him get orientated. He was crying and trying to get out of bed. I started to cry too. I did my best to not let my crying get in the way of helping my son. He began to calm down and was cleared to go back to his pre-surgery room and prepare to go home. As he was being wheeled out of post-op, he began singing, "Rolling, rolling, rolling, rolling, keep them doggies rolling, rawhide." I remember thinking, *My Zachariah is back*. He had cleared post-op and was shortly discharged from the hospital. We left the hospital that morning prepared to resume our lives together. We had purchased some of his favorite foods and a movie for him to watch.

On the way home, his pain intensified. He always had a high tolerance for pain, and we assumed that the pain was congruent with postsurgery. We got him home, and his pain continued, so we called back to the hospital and spoke with his surgeon. He instructed us to increase his pain medicine, believing his pain was associated with the surgery. While holding Zachariah as he lay on the couch, he told me he didn't think he could do this. I told him he was a warrior and it was going to be okay. I helped him walk over to the table so he could eat one of his favorite meals. We walked back to the couch, where Marchelle lay with him while he fell asleep. His heartbeat was strong and seemed to be resting. Marchelle slept with him that night, and I got up several times to check on him. Early the next morning, his heart stopped beating.

> We are called to a place where a deeper work in our heart is called for if we are to be able to continue our spiritual journey. It is in this desert experience of the heart where we are stripped of the protective clothing of the roles we have played, healing, repentance and faith are called for in ways we have not known previously. At this place in our journey, we face a wide and deep chasm that refuses us passage through self effort. It is in this place that truth eradicates the final heart walls and obstacles that separate us from the experience of surrender.
>
> (John Eldredge)

One of two things will rise up out of my pain: either a faith in something that seeks to deny my loss, therefore separating me from myself, or a faith in something that carries me back to my value. Thomas Chalmers writes in his sermon *Expulsive Power of a New Affection*, "The best way of casting out an impure affection is to admit a pure one. There is no personal transformation in which the heart is left without an object of ultimate beauty and joy. The heart's desire for one particular object can be conquered, but its desire to have some object is unconquerable."

When Zachariah first came into our lives, he resisted being held. He was fearful and confused. He would often resist being held and would become agitated when we attempted to comfort him. The abuse and neglect he had suffered damaged his willingness to trust. He believed that to expose his need would result in further hurt. What he needed most was what he feared the most. We witnessed the slow evolving and transforming power of what it means to let go and be held on to. As he began to believe, we saw physical and emotional change. His body was more relaxed, his eyes would look at us rather than look away, and he began to smile.

I press on, letting go yet holding on. I no longer cling to what I have lost and will ultimately lose. My grip is different. There is less fear and more acceptance. I seek to no longer hold on but to finally be held on to. Surrender requires this, and a meaningful life is dependent upon it. There is much that pushes against the idea of surrender. Maturation often is disproportionately weighted in what is logical, in what we can understand, control, and even dominate. The consequences of this perspective on living is that we lose touch with what it means to believe, trust, and depend. If I am to suffer well, I must let go in order to be held on to, even though the idea of being held goes against what we often think of as being strong.

EPILOGUE

I thought I saw Zachariah last night. I don't really believe I saw him, but for a second, something inside of me thought I did. It was a crowded room, and it must have been someone who looked like him. In that second, I felt this joy rise up within me. It was as if my body got out in front of reality. In that moment, I experienced an incredible joy. This kind of experience is also happening within my dreams. There is this reunification that words cannot describe. I am counting on heaven being that experience.

It has now been five years since his passing, and it can still be hard to believe. Thankfully, I have more acceptance today that he is gone. Finding acceptance has been a hard-fought battle, and the war is not over. I can't imagine never missing Zachariah, but the pain is lessening. Right after his passing, I was terrified my grief would overtake me. I was fearful to close my eyes or be still because of what the pain might do to me.

Marchelle and I are beginning to find comfort in conversations about our memories of Zachariah.—the trips we took, the funny moments, and the tender ones. It hurts, but I am learning that it cannot hurt too much. For it to hurt too much, I would have to stop believing in the grace that supplies the redemptive power of God's healing. It cannot hurt too much because this is not the end of the story. I must walk in the right direction, toward my understanding and belief in mercy. My new normal must involve a deeper understanding of this mercy and a more intimate trust in the mystery. I have discovered that mercy does exist in the midst of devastating loss. My comfort and security can no longer be dependent on what I once attempted to hold on to. Life is hard, and there is suffering all around me, yet mercy lives on.

Simone Weil, the French philosopher and Christian mystic, was right when she wrote, "There are only two things that pierce the human heart: beauty and affliction. Moments that we wish would last forever and moments we wish had never begun." There are so many memories; some filled with beauty and some with affliction. Beautiful moments filled with joy and laughter, and moments of sadness and fear. Multiple surgeries, watching people stare at him because of his compromised speech, sadness that I felt when I reflected on the abuse he had suffered or when I projected into the future knowing he would never be married or have children. Then the unimaginable: watching him pass away. My heart has been pierced by both beauty and great affliction.

My story is not unique. To truly live this life, our hearts will be pierced. The heart, both in the beauty and the affliction, longs for something greater, something that requires faith. We need a source that fills the empty space where the heart is pierced. A source that expands the heart by filling it with purpose and meaning. What fills the pierced heart will determine how we live life. There are many things in life requiring faith, and loss may be at the top of the list. My pierced heart is being filled with a comfort that at times can be difficult to explain. It truly is a peace that surpasses understanding. My pain can seem unbearable, and when I am in that place, the God of my understanding carries me through.

I have a blessed life for which I am so grateful, particularly in light of the loss that I carry. Any blessed life has to hold a space for loss. Being receptive to blessing must not be dependent on circumstances if it is to hold a place of substance. Some of the most powerful and deepest blessings have occurred as I grieve the loss of my son. I am reminded of a beautiful song called "Blessings" by Laura Story.

> What if your blessings come through raindrops?
> What if Your healing comes through tears?

> What if a thousand sleepless nights are what it takes to know You're near?
> What if trials of this life are Your mercies in disguise?
> What if my greatest disappointments
> Or the aching of this life
> Is the revealing of a greater thirst this world can't satisfy?

What beautiful words. There are clearly things this world cannot satisfy. The longings within my grief cry out for a supernatural intervention. My comfort and freedom require something so much bigger and greater than what I or any other person could supply. Without any doubt, I know I have reached for and been held on to by something greater that holds such power and beauty that words cannot adequately describe it. The language of my understanding utters words such as *grace* and *faith*. These words point me toward what I ultimately understand to be God—something divine and sacred that does not require my understanding but requires my trust. These kinds of thoughts stretch us to think and believe beyond what is believable. It is only through faith that the unbelievable becomes believable. My faith stretches beyond what I can see, feel, or touch. "I can't, but God can" has become a living, breathing part of my narrative. I choose to trust in an afterlife and look forward to the day when I will be reunited with my son.

Our deepest wounds are spiritual. We are created to love and trust. When this is violated, there is a profound injury that impacts our ability to believe. Heart resignation is the acceptance that this loss is final. Because of this belief of finality, there can be no faith experience. The risk involved is great, and the cost is believed to be too high. Hope is marginalized, and control is at a premium. When Zachariah was found by the police and social workers, he was taken to a hospital, treated, and eventually diagnosed as a "failure to thrive" baby. His body and his spirit had begun to shut down. This was due to the physical trauma he had suffered, but it was also due to the damage done to his spirit. His world had failed him. The breath and security necessary for living had not shown up. Faith and hope had not been delivered.

Life is moving on. I have watched as others have suffered, and my view of it is so different on this side of my loss. I pray my compassion is deeper today. Through my suffering, God has done some good work. I am different today, and I am grateful. I am also the same. Pride, envy, fear have returned, but even those things are different. They don't hold the same power, and they don't seem to stay as long.

It seems that right after Zachariah's passing, God picked me up and said, "I will carry you until it's time to walk on your own." He gently put me down and is now walking with me. I miss the days he was carrying me; I miss the freedom it provided. I am still free, but I can easily lose sight of it. For a brief time, it was almost as if I was not living in this world. The devastating loss had delivered me into the intimate and protective arms of God. I don't believe this side of heaven is meant for us to live in that place ... but someday I will live there forever. Until that day, I will do my best to live as God would have me live. Death cannot and will not have the final say. My God and my son are too important for death to be victorious. So I carry on, and because of God's grace, I will suffer well and live well. It is not finished.

> Stand at the crossroads and look. Ask for the ancient paths, the tried and true road. Then take it and you will find rest for your souls. (Jeremiah 6:16)

ABOUT THE AUTHOR

Fred Hampton is a therapist with over thirty years of experience working with the broken hearted. He is also a grieving father who writes from both a professional and very personal perspective. His commitment to suffering well is evident in the stories he shares and his insights into holding space for both grief and joy. Fred lives with his wife of forty one years along with his two dogs and two chickens. He is the father of three and the grandfather of six.